GLASS
PAINTING
DESIGNS

GLASS PAINTING DESIGNS

JANET EADIE

Kangaroo Press

ACKNOWLEDGMENTS

Thank you to my family, Alex, Laura and Evonne, for their encouragement, suggestions and support.

And thank you yet again, Steve Palin, for your helpfulness, and your step-by-step photography featured throughout this book.

I would also like to thank the following people:

David Sievers at Aspect Photographics Pty Ltd, Adelaide, South Australia, for the wonderful photographs of the finished projects.

Dave Fyfe from The Tin Shed, McLaren Vale, South Australia, for the custom-made frames.

Express Publications for permission to use the Lemon and Pear frames featured previously in *Craft and Decorating* magazine.

DMC (Australia) Pty Ltd for supplying paint (Plaid Gallery Glass Window Colour).

Finmark Découpage for permission to use their découpage paper on the Mermaid Frame.

GLASS PAINTING DESIGNS

First published in Australia in 2000 by Kangaroo Press
An imprint of Simon & Schuster (Aust.) Pty Ltd
20 Barcoo Street, East Roseville NSW 2069

A Viacom Company
Sydney New York London Toronto Tokyo Singapore

© Janet Eadie 2000

National Library of Australia
Cataloguing-in-Publication data

Eadie, Janet.
Glass painting designs.

Includes index.
ISBN 0 7318 0922 X.

1. Glass painting and staining - Patterns.
2. Glass craft - Patterns. I. Title.

748.50284

Cover and internal design: Anna Soo, Anna Soo Designs
Internal design: Anna Soo, Anna Soo Designs
Photographers: David Sievers and Steve Palin

Set in Sabon 11.5/15 pt.
Printed in China by Everbest Printing Co.

10 9 8 7 6 5 4 3 2

CONTENTS

INTRODUCTION

My initial introduction to glass painting was through the promotion of Plaid Gallery Glass Window Colour paints in my work as a demonstrator with DMC (Australia) Pty Ltd. It always surprised me that the most frequent requests were for simple designs that would suit coffee jars and vases, and so I was encouraged to write a book of my own.

Glass painting has always had great appeal for me due to the clarity and freshness of colour revealed when the light shines through the transparent paint. Simple, uncomplicated designs lend themselves best to this form of painting, where the beauty lies in the reflected colour rather than in detail in the design.

While the projects featured in this book have been created with Plaid Window Colour paints, other glass paint mediums will suit some of the designs. I have included a colour conversion chart for Pebeo's Vitrail and Porcelaine 150 paints. Any of the designs can be enlarged or reduced on a photocopier to suit your needs.

Glass painting with Window Colour resembles leadlighting, with the advantage of being able to mix and swirl colours together so you can be very creative. The projects can be used to decorate windows and glass doors in your own home, to create colourful framed mirrors and pictures, and to make smaller decorative items such as vases, canisters and coffee jars for yourself or as gifts for your friends.

I have never tired of using and promoting this medium and have greatly enjoyed designing this collection of projects. I hope you will be inspired to create some for yourself.

EQUIPMENT AND MATERIALS

Plaid Gallery Glass Window Colour A water-based, non-toxic paint. When first applied it appears milky, but once dry this thick, textured paint has the appearance of textured stained glass. Because it is so thick, this paint can be applied to vertical and curved surfaces as well as to horizontal surfaces. It needs to be 'combed' through to distribute the paint evenly, which gives it a slightly textured finish. The beauty of this paint is that there is no need for kiln firing. The paint will remain permanent, but can be removed if necessary using a scalpel or craft knife (see below).

For a smoother, finer paint finish, the Window Colour paint can be warmed by sitting the tubes in a cup of hot (not boiling) water. This makes the paint more fluid and, by combing through it with a pin, the dried paint surface will be less textured. I have used this technique on the vases, canisters and suncatchers.

Other paints While I have used Window Colour for the projects in this book, a lot of the designs will suit other glass paints on the market, such as Pebeo Vitrail and Pebeo Porcelaine 150.

Gallery Glass Liquid Leading A water-based thick paint, used to outline the design. It resembles the lead used in leadlighting and helps to separate different coloured sections of your design. Available in 2, 4 and 8 oz bottles.

Tracing paper Trace all designs onto lightweight paper and then tape behind glass as a guide when outlining the design in Liquid Leading on the glass.

Pen Use a dark pen to trace out your design.

Skewer A metal skewer or large darning needle can be used to pierce the nozzle of the bottle of Liquid Leading.

Pin Necessary for bursting any large air bubbles that may form in the paint when it is applied. Longer quilting pins are ideal as they are easier to hold. Can be used to comb through paint for a finer finish.

Toothpicks Wooden toothpicks are used to mix colours and to push paint to meet the edge of leading outlines. They will not scratch the glass surface of your project.

Cotton buds Used to wipe away excess paint if errors occur in applying it.

Paper towels Used to wipe excess paint off nozzle during paint application.

Plastic A4 sleeves Available from most stationers or newsagents. These plastic folder inserts are perfect for holding a design under plastic and for creating the peel and press elements used in vertical paint application. They are also used for piping lines of leading. The slight texture on the surface of this plastic means the complete design will peel off with ease and can then be self-adhered to a glass surface.

A4 acetate This is available from stationers as overhead transparency sheets. It is used for the suncatchers on pages 52–56.

Lined paper A sheet of lined paper inside the plastic sleeve acts as a guide when you are piping leading strips in straight lines.

Scissors A small pair of nail scissors is used to snip leading to the correct length when creating vertical designs.

Scalpel or craft knife If it is necessary to remove any sections of dried paint, a scalpel or craft knife will cut close to the edge of leading so that the damaged area can be cut away. Be careful not to slice too heavily or glass may be scratched.

Sharpened eraser For removing small areas of wet leading or to make outlining more even. I have found an eraser cut to a point can be glided along the glass surface and will smoothly wipe away small mistakes in leading. Some art shops sell a special tool with a pointed rubber end, (shown in Figure 1 along with the other glass painting equipment) .

Sticky tape To allow leading to flow more smoothly, wind a length of sticky tape around the nozzle of the bottle after snipping off the tip of the nozzle.

12 mm (½ in) flat paintbrush I use this brush to paint in criss-cross strokes when I am applying Clear Frost Window Colour paint as a background. You can very quickly cover a large area with this method, used in the Pear and Cherry framed picture (Figure 14).

Varnish The use of varnish is only necessary where the painted surface will be exposed to a lot of moisture, for example, in a steamy bathroom, or on painted storage jars or vases. Make sure the varnish is compatible with the glass paint (do a test first). The varnish should preferably be a water-based spray, but on the coffee jars I have painted a liquid water-based varnish over the design. Instructions for applying varnish appear in the section on vases and canisters on pages 12 and 24.

Frames Make sure you choose frames where the glass is secured with metal clips which allow the glass to be removed and replaced. Remove the cardboard or wooden backing and paint the design on the glass out of the frame. When the paint has dried clip the glass back into the frame.

COLOUR CONVERSION CHART

There are other glass paints available which may suit some of the designs in this book. This chart lists the comparable colours available in other ranges.

Window Colour	Porcelaine 150 (Pebeo)	Vitrail (Pebeo)
Crystal Clear	—	—
Snow White	Ivory	White
Cameo Ivory	—	—
Sunny Yellow	Marseille Yellow	Lemon
Orange Poppy	Agate	Orange
Canyon Coral	—	—
Cocoa Brown	Light Scale Brown	Brown
Kelly Green	Olivine	Green Gold
Emerald Green	Amazonite	Emerald
Turquoise	Turquoise	Turquoise
Denim Blue	Haematite	—
Blue Diamond	Ming Blue	—
Royal Blue	Lapis	Deep Blue
Slate Blue	Petroleum Blue	—
Amethyst	Parma	—
Ruby Red	Tourmaline	Crimson
Rose Quartz	Opaline Pink	Pink
Magenta Royale	Amethyst	Violet
Charcoal Black	Abyss	Black
Gold Sparkle	Gold	—
Amber	Saffron	Yellow
White Pearl	—	—
Clear Frost	—	—
Berry Red	Etruscan Red	Red Violet
Ivy Green	Bronze	Chartreuse Green

TECHNIQUES

PREPARATION OF GLASS SURFACE

The glass surface must be free of dust and grease before you start to paint it. Use a soft cloth rinsed in soapy water to clean the glass, and another soft cloth, lint-free, to polish it dry.

If the decoration is to be applied to an existing window or door, work on the inside, as the paint cannot be exposed to the elements. Do not hang curtains too close to a painted door or window, as there needs to be a certain amount of air circulation around the painted surface. This is so that moisture will evaporate and not sit on the paintwork in wet weather.

PREPARING LIQUID LEADING

Liquid Leading is a non-toxic paint used to outline the design before colour is applied. The instructions on the bottle tell you to pierce a hole in the nozzle with a skewer and shake the contents to the tip. However, the best method I have found for squeezing out leading is to snip off a small portion of the nozzle and then to wind sticky tape around it (see Figure 2).

Place a 5 cm (2 in) length of sticky tape on an angle over the nozzle and wind it around. The tape will spiral upwards and then reverse down to the base of the nozzle. You can alter the thickness of the nozzle by altering the angle the tape is first placed on the nozzle. The more acute the angle at which the sticky tape is first positioned, the finer the hole in the nozzle.

I have found this method the easiest way to squeeze out leading and retain an even flow while outlining. The snipped tip allows the leading to flow out more smoothly. You will need to recap the bottle afterwards and apply a fresh nozzle each time you need to use leading.

Before outlining your design, assess how thick you want the leaded outline to be. As a general rule of thumb, the larger the project, the wider the leading should be, to create a pleasing balance. For smaller projects such as vases or coffee jars the reverse applies—make the leading finer the smaller the design.

If a particularly thick outline is required, simply snip a small portion off the nozzle and use the leading without the sticky tape extension.

Once the bottle is nearly empty, the amount of air inside it will cause the remaining leading to 'spatter' as you squeeze. I have found the best way to avoid this is to purchase a new bottle and, once you have used most of the leading in the old bottle, to squeeze the leftovers into the new bottle, most easily done by cutting the used one in half.

TIP Always shake the contents of the leading bottle to the tip before you start outlining.

OUTLINING THE DESIGN

Place the design behind the horizontal glass or plastic surface.

Hold the nozzle of the leading bottle slightly above the surface and, maintaining an even pressure on the bottle, allow the leading to 'drape' along the outline. This will give you a smoother outline than you will achieve by 'travelling' the nozzle firmly along the surface.

To break the flow of leading, stop squeezing the bottle and touch the nozzle to the surface.

Smooth any joins with a pin while leading is still wet.

Mistakes in your outlining can be removed by either of two methods.

The easier way (especially for larger areas) is to wait for the leading to dry and to snip off the offending section with a craft knife. Once the mistake is removed, a new line of leading can be applied and the joins smoothed over by using a pin.

You can remove minor imperfections in outlining or make a line more uniform by running the point of a sharpened eraser along the edge of wet leading. The eraser will glide smoothly along glass and make a straighter line.

MIXING COLOURS

Colours outside the manufacturer's range can be created by mixing paints together while still wet, provided paints are from the same range (e.g. Window Colour + Window Colour).

Simply squeeze a puddle of each of two different colours into the outlined area, then use a toothpick to swirl them together until they are completely mixed. Push the paint to meet the edge of the leading and 'comb' through to distribute the paint more evenly.

If you want a streaked effect, squeeze the two colours into the outlined section, but do not mix completely. Just use a toothpick or pin in a backward/forward motion to streak colours together.

To make a softer shade of a particular colour you can add either White or Crystal Clear to it and mix as described above. As an example, in the Large Fish Frame (Figure 19), I have toned down the Emerald Green in some of the reeds by mixing Snow White with the Emerald Green.

If a very large area is to be covered with mixed Window Colours, you will find it easier to pre-mix the paint in the bottle. Remove the nozzle from one of the bottles and squeeze in the required amount of the second colour. Stir the paint well with a skewer before replacing the nozzle. Avoid shaking vigorously, as this can create excess air bubbles.

MARBLING

An interesting finish is created by only partly swirling two colours together in an outlined section before pushing the paint to meet the edge of leading. If you avoid combing through the paint, the finished effect will be more marbled than solid.

DIMENSIONAL FABRIC PAINT DETAIL

You can add fine detail to many designs with dimensional fabric paint. Allow the glass paint to cure for 5 to 7 days before painting in the detail. As fabric paint is solid in texture, it can give interesting contrasts of detail over the translucent glass paint.

CLEANING

Allow the paint to cure for a week before cleaning by wiping over with a soft moist cloth. Do not use excessive water, solvent-based cleaners or any abrasive cloth.

PROBLEM SOLVING

♦ There will be times when you are unhappy with an area of your design and want to remove it. Allow the paint to dry, then cut as close to the edge of the leading as possible using a scalpel or craft knife. The problem area can then be peeled off in a complete section and a new colour applied.

♦ Lots of air bubbles? Avoid shaking bottles of paint, as this can create excessive bubbles in paint. Once paint has been applied, you can use a pin to burst bubbles within a period of approximately 20 minutes.

♦ If the leading outline is uneven, or 'wobbly', you may be squeezing the bottle unevenly, or moving more slowly in some sections. Both will create wider lines in the leading. Wait until the leading has dried, then cut away the problem area with a craft knife. Re-apply leading to that section, smoothing over joins while they are wet with a pin.

♦ Enlarged joins in leading where lines meet? Try to stop squeezing the bottle of leading just before reaching the point where lines overlap, and touch the nozzle to the surface to stop the flow of leading. Smooth joins with a pin while leading is wet.

♦ The liquid leading curves around the nozzle as you start to squeeze the bottle? Wipe the nozzle clean with paper towel, then, as you first squeeze the bottle, touch to the surface to anchor the leading before lifting slightly to continue outlining.

♦ Uneven colour when paint has dried? This means the paint is thicker in some places than others. Make sure you comb through the wet paint to distribute it evenly.

♦ Light holes in the dried paint? If the paint is not pushed completely up to the lines of leading, you will see gaps in your work when it has dried. Simply pick up a small amount of paint on the end of a toothpick and fill in these areas. Once dry, it will blend with existing paint.

♦ Paint appears cloudy? Window Colour will always appear cloudy when the paint is wet, but will dry to a transparent finish. Wait for a dry day to apply paint to your project as moisture trapped beneath the paint will remain there and cause a cloudy effect. High levels of humidity in the air can sometimes make this paint resume its cloudy state, after the paint has dried.

♦ Crystal Clear Window Colour, applied very thickly, will sometimes remain slightly cloudy in some areas, but the overall effect will be a clear, transparent paint. Avoid unwanted cloudiness by distributing the wet paint thoroughly.

♦ Paint running off a vertical surface? This indicates that too much paint has been applied. Use less paint in the lower sections of the design to allow for it to 'drop' slightly. Leave approximately 10–15 mm (¼–½ in) clear space above the bottom line of leading in any section of a vertical design and push the paint from above the space to meet leading.

♦ Blockage in paint tube? Sometimes a lump may form within a Window Colour paint tube which interferes with the flow of paint through the nozzle. Remove the nozzle (by pushing it sideways) and poke a toothpick through the nozzle to unblock it or remove any hardened paint. Push the nozzle firmly back into place.

APPLYING A DESIGN

There are two ways of applying your design to a glass surface. Which one you use depends on whether the surface is horizontal, vertical or curved.

DIRECT APPLICATION (HORIZONTAL METHOD)

If the project can be laid flat, the leading can be piped directly from the bottle onto the project to outline the design. Once dry, Window Colour is applied into each outlined section and left to dry to a transparent finish. I have used this method on the frames, the canisters, the Moccona coffee jars and the vases.

Leading Tape the design under the glass and use Liquid Leading to outline the design, following the instructions on page 5. Once you are satisfied with the outline, set aside to dry for 24 to 48 hours, until firm to the touch.

Window Colour paints Apply colour into each outlined section by squeezing paint directly from the bottle and use the nozzle to push paint to meet the edge of leading. Make sure that paint touches leading on all edges, as this seals the leading onto the glass. It may at first look slightly untidy if the paint goes onto the leading, but once the paint has dried to a transparent finish it will not be noticeable, and you will only see a continuous, even line of leading.

If the paint does not meet the leading, you will have light holes in your design. This can be touched up with fresh paint at a later stage.

Comb through the wet paint to distribute it more evenly. Use a toothpick with a backward/forward motion.

If there are any air bubbles, use a pin to burst them. Some bubbles are quite stubborn, and you will need to burst them within the first 20 minutes. After this time a skin will begin to form on the paint surface.

Where a more textured background is required, such as with the Crystal Clear Window Colour, apply the paint, spread it to meet the edge of the leading and then wait for 5–10 minutes, until the paint has thickened slightly. Use a toothpick to either swirl or draw figure eights through the wet paint. Once the paint is dry, this textured background adds contrast to smoother areas.

Allow the painted project to lie flat for 24 to 48 hours while drying. The length of drying time will depend on the amount of humidity in the air. The Crystal Clear background can sometimes remain cloudy for several weeks or become cloudy if a lot of moisture is in the air.

Window Colour paint will dry deeper in colour than it appears in the bottle.

VERTICAL APPLICATION

Firstly, assess your design to decide which areas can be applied directly to the vertical surface with leading strips, and which need to be individually worked on a flat plastic surface using the peel and press technique. An example of this is the Large Fish Frame, on page 31, where the fish, shells and bubbles are worked on plastic as peel and press elements (see figures 5–9). The remainder of the design (the reeds) is outlined with dry leading strips (see below).

Peel and press method The peel and press method, for Liquid Leading and Window Colour paints, is used where the area to be decorated is in a fixed vertical position (such as an existing window or door). The required elements of the design are first worked onto A4 plastic sleeves. When completely dry, they are peeled off the plastic and will self-adhere to the vertical glass surface. The remainder of the design can be connected using pre-piped leading strips. Any background area can be painted onto the upright surface using Window Colour. Most of the designs in this book can be worked in this way.

The A4 plastic sleeves sold at most newsagents and stationers are perfect for working the peel and press technique. The slight texture on the plastic surface allows you to peel off the paint in a complete piece.

Insert the design inside the plastic sleeve and pipe the outline in leading. Allow to dry for 24 to 48 hours before squeezing Window Colour into each section. Spread the paint to meet the edges of leading, then comb through to distribute more evenly. Burst any air bubbles if necessary. Set aside to dry for approximately another 24 to 48 hours.

Clean the glass on the surface to be decorated to remove any grease and dust. **Do not** use any solvent cleaners, just a cloth rung out in soapy water. Use a soft lint-free cloth to polish dry. Tape the design behind the glass.

Peel the dry elements of the design off the plastic sleeve and press firmly onto the glass surface in the correct position. Apply pressure at the top and gradually push out any air from underneath the design. Once all peel and press elements are in place you can use dry leading strips to complete the design.

Leading strips Insert a sheet of lined paper inside a plastic sleeve and lay it on a flat surface. Pipe Liquid Leading lines in the desired thickness along the plastic, using the lined paper as a guide. Let the leading drape onto the plastic by holding the nozzle slightly above the surface. This will give you a smoother line than if you pipe with the nozzle touching the surface.

If lines are not all continuous, don't worry, as some areas of design will require shorter lengths. Allow these lines to dry for 24 to 48 hours until they will peel off the plastic easily.

Snip off any enlarged ends from the leading strips and press onto the clean glass surface following the outline of your design. These strips are self-adhering, but can be repositioned if necessary. Avoid stretching the leading lines when applying to glass.

As you apply the strips to your design, use your fingernail to make an indentation at the exact point you need to cut. A small pair of nail scissors can be used to snip leading. **Do not** leave any overlaps, as the dried leading will not adhere to itself.

If you have cut the strip of leading a little too short, you can squeeze a dot of leading straight from the tube to join the lines together. It is a good idea to squeeze leading dots over all joins to seal the outlining completely.

Background paint Once the peel and press elements are in place and the leading lines have been applied to complete your design, you can apply the background colour directly onto the upright glass panel. Background paint can be applied to the upright glass surface straight from the bottle of Window Colour.

Start at one of the upper corners and run the nozzle backwards and forwards until the area is covered. Make sure you push paint to meet the edges of the leading to properly seal the leading strips to the window.

As you reach the bottom of each section, use less paint to allow for a slight 'drop' as it dries. If you find paint running over the edge of leading, stop applying paint approximately 10–15 mm (¼–²/₃ in) short of the lower edge and push the existing paint to meet the lower edge using a toothpick.

For a smooth background colour you will need to comb through each section with a toothpick.

For a textured background in Crystal Clear Window Colour use a toothpick to draw swirls or figure eights in wet paint. The texture will be more noticeable when the paint has dried.

For a very quick, slightly frosted background, Clear Frost Window Colour can be applied using a paintbrush.

First, squeeze a puddle of paint onto a tile or plastic plate and pick up some paint on a 12 mm (½ in) flat paintbrush.

Apply paint to the background area using short crisscross strokes. Brush paint slightly over the edge of all leading to be sure leading is well sealed. This is an extremely quick and easy method of applying a background to a large project.

See the Pear and Cherry Frame (Figure 14), where Clear Frost has been applied to the lower section.

FIGURE 1: The materials and equipment needed for glass painting are basic, and few in number

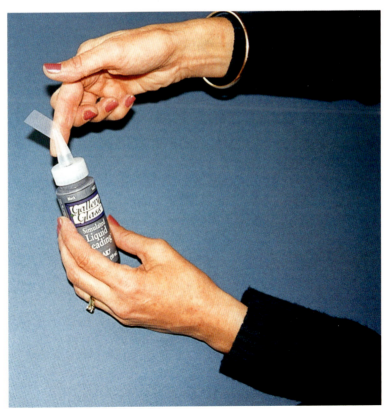

FIGURE 2: Making a sticky tape extension for the nozzle of a liquid leading bottle

FIGURE 3: Applying details to bottlebrush flower in dimensional paint

FIGURE 4: Removing unwanted paint: cut against leading and peel away dry paint

FIGURE 5: The first step in creating a peel and press design—outlining the design on an A4 plastic sleeve

FIGURE 6: Blending paint with a toothpick

FIGURE 7: Peeling the completed peel and press element from the plastic backing

FIGURE 8: Positioning the peel and press element on the glass, with the design outline laid under the glass as a guide

PROJECTS

VASES

These rectangular glass vases, approximately 10 cm wide and 7 cm deep (4 in × 3 in) and of varying heights, are perfect for decorating with glass paint. Either functional or used as ornaments, they look stunning on shelves with light reflecting through them. Similar vases are readily available from the glassware section in most department stores.

I have created a finer appearance by sitting the paint tubes in a cup of hot water before use, making the paint more fluid and easier to spread, and combing through with a pin to avoid a textured finish.

If the vases are to be functional, the fully cured paint will need to be protected with a spray of varnish, preferably a water-based spray varnish which is compatible with glass paint. Do a test check first. Wait one or two weeks for the paint to fully cure before you varnish.

Mask off the areas surrounding the paintwork by cutting a hole in a sheet of cardboard slightly larger than the painted design. Lay cardboard over the top of your design and give two light mists of varnish, drying well between coats. This will give added protection to your paint when the vase is cleaned (see Figure 12).

Do not soak vases in water or use solvent cleaners. Wipe clean with a soft cloth wrung out in soapy water.

> **TIP** If the design you want to use is too large or too small for the vase you have chosen to decorate, bless the day the photocopier was invented, and just enlarge or reduce the design to fit.

IRIS VASE

Illustrated in Figure 15
MATERIALS
rectangular vase approx. 22 x 10 cm (8½ x 4 in)
Plaid Gallery Glass Liquid Leading:
  Soft Black
  Plaid Gallery Glass Window Colour:
  Amethyst
  Sunny Yellow
  Emerald Green
  Ivy Green
  Crystal Clear
  Kelly Green
plastic grocery bags
greaseproof paper
pin
paper towels
toothpick
water-based spray varnish

METHOD
Trace design onto greaseproof paper and cut to fit inside vase. Use several plastic grocery bags to pad design up to meet surface inside vase.

Lay vase on a flat surface and outline design in Liquid Leading. Allow to dry for approximately 24 hours.

Apply Window Colour into individual outlined sections in the following order, referring to photo for colour placement.

ABOVE: Vase designs: Iris (page 12), Morning Glory (page 17), Small Blue Violet (page 15).
ENLARGE AT 200%

BELOW: Vase designs: Daffodil (page16), Pink Violet (page 15), Rose (page 14). **ENLARGE AT 200%**

Petals Apply Amethyst to most of the lower three petals, leaving centre free of Amethyst paint. Apply Sunny Yellow in the centre of petals and use a pin to blend slightly. Comb through each section with a pin for a smooth finish.

The two upper petals are painted with Amethyst. Comb through with a pin.

Leaves and stem Use Emerald Green and Ivy Green for the leaves and stem. Comb through with a pin.

Background Apply equal amounts of Crystal Clear and Kelly Green in each section and mix with a toothpick. Comb through with a pin.

If any air bubbles appear, use a pin to burst them, allowing approximately 20 minutes for some stubborn bubbles to burst. After this time a skin may begin to form on paint.

Set aside to dry on a flat surface and allow several weeks to fully cure. If necessary, spray with a mist of water-based varnish as described above.

ROSE VASE

Illustrated in Figure 15

MATERIALS

rectangular vase approx. 22 x 10 cm (8½ x 4 in)
Plaid Gallery Glass Liquid Leading:
  Soft Black
  Plaid Gallery Glass Window Colour:
  Ruby Red
  Kelly Green
  Emerald Green
  Crystal Clear
plastic grocery bags
greaseproof paper
pin
toothpick
water-based spray varnish

METHOD

Trace design onto greaseproof paper and cut to fit inside vase.

Use several plastic grocery bags to pad design up to meet surface inside vase.

Lay vase on a flat surface and outline design in Liquid Leading. Allow to dry for approximately 24 hours.

Apply Window Colour into individual outlined sections in the following order, referring to photo for colour placement.

Petals For lighter petals use Crystal Clear with a touch of Ruby Red picked up on the end of a toothpick. Swirl together to make a soft pink. For a slightly stronger pink colour, add a touch more Ruby Red to Crystal Clear and swirl together with a toothpick to combine colour. For the darkest petals use Ruby Red. Comb through with a pin.

Leaves and stem Use Kelly Green for the lighter half of leaf. For the stem and darker side of leaf, use Emerald Green. Comb through with a pin.

Background Paint the four side sections with a mix of Crystal Clear and a touch of Emerald Green (4:1). For the top and bottom sections, mix Crystal Clear and Emerald Green at 3:1. The centre diamond is left free of paint.

If any air bubbles appear, use a pin to burst them, allowing approximately 20 minutes for some stubborn bubbles to burst. After this time a skin may begin to form on paint.

Set aside to dry on a flat surface and allow several weeks to fully cure. If necessary, spray with a mist of water-based varnish as described above.

PINK VIOLET VASE

MATERIALS
rectangular vase approx. 22 x 10 cm (8½ x 4 in)
Plaid Gallery Glass Liquid Leading:
  Soft Black
Plaid Gallery Glass Window Colour:
  Amethyst
  Magenta Royale
  Turquoise
  Emerald Green
  Kelly Green
plastic grocery bags
greaseproof paper
pin
water-based spray varnish

METHOD
Trace design onto greaseproof paper, and cut to fit inside vase.

Use several plastic grocery bags to pad design up to meet surface inside vase.

Lay vase on a flat surface and outline design in Liquid Leading. Allow to dry for approximately 24 hours.

Apply Window Colour into individual outlined sections in the following order, referring to the Figure 15 for colour placement.

Petals The upper two petals on each flower are Amethyst. Comb through with a pin. The lower three petals on each flower are Magenta Royale with a few drops of Amethyst added at centre of flower. Use a pin to streak colour outwards.

Leaves Use Kelly Green on one side of leaf and Emerald Green on other half of leaf. Comb through with a pin.

Background Colour three of the background areas with Turquoise, following the photo. Comb through with a pin. Leave the remainder of background free of paint.

If any air bubbles appear, use a pin to burst them, allowing approximately 20 minutes for some stubborn bubbles to burst. After this time a skin may begin to form on paint.

Set aside to dry on a flat surface and allow several weeks to fully cure.

If necessary, spray with a mist of water-based varnish as described above.

SMALL BLUE VIOLET VASE

MATERIALS
rectangular vase approx. 18 x 10 cm (7 in x 4 in)
Plaid Gallery Glass Liquid Leading:
  Soft Black
Plaid Gallery Glass Window Colour:
  Blue Diamond
  Amethyst
  Royal Blue
  Kelly Green
  Emerald Green
  Crystal Clear
plastic grocery bags
greaseproof paper
pin
toothpick
water-based spray varnish

METHOD

Trace design onto greaseproof paper, adapting spaces between flowers as necessary and making the background divisions diagonal instead of square, and cut to fit inside vase.

Use several plastic grocery bags to pad design up to meet surface inside vase.

Lay vase on a flat surface and outline design in Liquid Leading. Allow to dry for approximately 24 hours.

Apply Window Colour into individual outlined sections in the following order, referring to photo for colour placement.

Petals Use Blue Diamond on the upper two petals. Comb through with a pin.

Use Blue Diamond on the lower three petals as well as a few drops of Royal Blue on the larger petal. Squeeze Amethyst into the centre of the three lower petals and blend slightly outwards with a pin.

Background The top and bottom triangles are painted with a mix of equal amounts Crystal Clear and Blue Diamond. The four side triangles are painted with a mix of 2 parts Crystal Clear and 1 part Blue Diamond. Combine colours with a toothpick. Comb through with a pin.

Leaves Refer to Pink Violet Vase.

If any air bubbles appear, use a pin to burst them, allowing approximately 20 minutes for some stubborn bubbles to burst. After this time a skin may begin to form on paint.

Set aside to dry on a flat surface and allow several weeks to fully cure. If necessary, spray with a mist of water-based varnish as described above.

DAFFODIL VASE

Illustrated in Figure 15

MATERIALS
rectangular vase approx. 24 x 10 cm (9½ x 4 in)
Plaid Gallery Glass Liquid Leading:
  Soft Black
Plaid Gallery Glass Window Colour:
  Sunny Yellow
  Kelly Green
  Ivy Green
  Orange Poppy
  Crystal Clear
plastic grocery bags
greaseproof paper
pin
toothpick
water-based spray varnish

METHOD
Trace design onto greaseproof paper and cut to fit inside vase.

Use several plastic grocery bags to pad design up to meet surface inside vase.

Lay vase on a flat surface and outline design in Liquid Leading. Allow to dry for approximately 24 hours.

Apply Window Colour into individual outlined sections in the following order, referring to photo for colour placement. Complete each section before moving to the next, if mixing colours together.

Petals Squeeze Sunny Yellow into each petal and add a few drops of Orange Poppy to create shading where petals overlap. While paint is still wet, use a pin to swirl together. Comb through with a pin.

Leaves and stem Use Kelly Green for one side of each leaf and Ivy Green for the other side of each leaf and the stem. Comb through with a pin.

Background Refer to tFigure 15 and use an equal mix of Crystal Clear and Kelly Green to paint the three background areas, combine colours with a toothpick and leave remainder free of paint. Comb through with a pin.

If any air bubbles appear, use a pin to burst them, allowing approximately 20 minutes for some stubborn bubbles to burst. After this time a skin may begin to form on paint.

Set aside to dry on a flat surface and allow several weeks to fully cure.

If necessary, spray with a mist of water-based varnish as described above.

MORNING GLORY VASE

Illustrated in Figure 15
MATERIALS
rectangular vase approx. 22 x 10 cm (8½ in x 4 in)
Plaid Gallery Glass Liquid Leading:
  Soft Black
Plaid Gallery Glass Window Colour:
  Blue Diamond
  Amethyst
  Turquoise
  Emerald Green
  Kelly Green
plastic grocery bags
greaseproof paper
pin
toothpick
spray varnish, water-based

METHOD
Trace design onto greaseproof paper and cut to fit inside vase.

Use several plastic groceryg bags to pad design up to meet surface inside vase.

Lay vase on a flat surface and outline design in Liquid Leading. Allow to dry for approximately 24 hours.

Apply Window Colour into individual outlined sections in the following order, referring to photo for colour placement. Complete each section before moving to next, if mixing colours together.

Flowers Paint Blue Diamond over outer flower area. Apply Amethyst in the centre of flower and use a pin to streak colour outwards slightly. Mix Amethyst and Blue Diamond together for lower tube of flower, combining colours with a toothpick. Comb through with a pin.

Leaves and stems Use Emerald Green to paint the top half of both leaves. Use Kelly Green to paint lower leaf section and the stems of the flower. Comb through with a pin.

Background Leave the centre diamond area free of paint. Use Turquoise to paint the upper and lower background section. Comb through with a pin. The side panels of background are painted in Amethyst. Comb through with a pin.

If any air bubbles appear, use a pin to burst them, allowing approximately 20 minutes for some stubborn bubbles to burst. After this time a skin may begin to form on paint.

Set aside to dry on a flat surface and allow several weeks to fully cure.

If necessary, spray with a mist of water-based varnish as described above.

MOCCONA COFFEE JARS

These attractively shaped coffee jars make excellent storage jars or a colourful display in any kitchen. The designs featured here suit medium and large Moccona coffee jars. To get rid of the extremely tenacious remainders of the sticky label on the rim and the lid, soak the jars in hot soapy water, then rub with a metal pot scourer. Eucalyptus oil will remove any residual stickiness.

Trace the design onto greaseproof paper and insert it into the jar. The best way to hold the traced design in place is to pad inside the jar with crumpled plastic grocery bags so the greaseproof paper is pressed up against the glass. This way you can position the design correctly without trying to use sticky tape to hold it in place (very awkward).

Lay the jar on its side on a work surface, with a fat book or something similar on either side to hold it steady while you outline the design in the Liquid Leading.

Allow the painted design to cure for a week before sealing the surface, if necessary. Use a water-based varnish which will be compatible with the paint. I prefer Cabot's Crystal Clear varnish. Using a soft flat brush, paint over the design, coming just slightly outside the leading to protect the surface from moisture. You could also use a water-based spray varnish as I suggested for the flat-sided vases, but it will be more difficult to mask off the surrounding area on the curved jar.

Do not soak painted jars in water or wash in a dishwasher. To clean, wipe over with a soft cloth, wrung out in soapy water.

PINK POPPY JAR

Illustrated in Figure 17
MATERIALS
large Moccona coffee jar
Plaid Gallery Glass Liquid Leading:
  Soft Black
Plaid Gallery Glass Window Colour:
  Berry Red
  Denim Blue
  White Pearl
  Emerald Green
3 or 4 plastic grocery bags
toothpick
pin
greaseproof paper
water-based varnish (e.g. Cabot's Crystal Clear)
brush, 12 mm (½ in) flat

METHOD
Trace design onto greaseproof paper and cut out. Insert in jar and pad against surface with crumpled plastic grocery bags.

Lay jar flat to pipe on leading design and allow to dry for approximately 12 to 24 hours.

Apply Window Colour in following sequence, using the photo for guidance.

Petals Colour the three back petals with Berry Red. Use a toothpick to push the paint into place between the dots of leading, making sure paint touches the leading outline. The front petal has Berry Red applied at the base, reaching halfway up petal. At the top of petal use White Pearl. To

ABOVE: Jar designs: Pink Poppy (page 18), Yellow Tulip (page 20), Purple-Blue Daisy (page 21). **ENLARGE AT 151%**

BELOW: Jar designs: Small Red Daisy (page 21), Blue Flower (page 22), Small Daffodil (page 23). **ENLARGE AT 151%**

blend the two colours, use a pin in a backwards and forwards motion to slightly combine the paint. This will add highlight to front petal.

Stem and side panels Paint with Emerald Green. Comb through with a pin.

Background Paint with Denim Blue. Comb through with a pin.

Use a pin to burst any larger air bubbles. Leave jar lying flat to dry for 12 to 24 hours. If the jar is to be used and will require washing from time to time, protect the design with a coat of varnish as described on page 18.

YELLOW TULIP JAR

Illustrated in Figure 17

MATERIALS
large Moccona coffee jar
Plaid Gallery Glass Liquid Leading:
  Soft Black
Plaid Gallery Glass Window Colour:
  Sunny Yellow
  Amber
  Emerald Green
  Kelly Green
  Crystal Clear
3 or 4 plastic grocery bags
toothpick
pin
greaseproof paper
water-based varnish (e.g. Cabot's Crystal
  Clear)
brush, 12 mm (½ in) flat

METHOD
Trace design onto greaseproof paper and cut out. Insert in jar and pad against surface with crumpled plastic grocery bags.

Lay jar flat to pipe on leading design and allow to dry for approximately 12 to 24 hours.

Apply Window Colour in following sequence, using the photo for guidance.

Petals Apply Amber at the base of the front two tulip petals and use Sunny Yellow over the remaining parts of petals. While paint is still wet use a pin to streak these colours slightly together to create a little shading on tulip.

Leaves and stems Paint in Emerald Green.

Background A soft green created by mixing 3 parts Crystal Clear and 1 part Kelly Green together within each section. Combine colours with a toothpick. Comb through with a pin.

Side panels Paint with Kelly Green. Comb through with a pin.

Use a pin to burst any larger air bubbles. Leave jar lying flat to dry for 12 to 24 hours. If the jar is to be used and will require washing from time to time, protect the design with a coat of varnish as described on page 18.

PURPLE-BLUE DAISY JAR

Illustrated in Figure 17

MATERIALS

large Moccona coffee jar
Plaid Gallery Glass Liquid Leading:
  Soft Black
Plaid Gallery Glass Window Colour:
  Blue Diamond
  Royal Blue
  Amethyst
  Kelly Green
  Emerald Green
  Magenta Royale
3 or 4 plastic grocery bags
pin
greaseproof paper
water-based varnish (e.g. Cabot's Crystal
  Clear)
brush, 12 mm (½ in) flat

METHOD

Trace design onto greaseproof paper and cut out. Insert in jar and pad against surface with crumpled plastic grocery bags.

Lay jar flat to pipe on leading design and allow to dry for approximately 12 to 24 hours.

Apply Window Colour in following sequence, using the photo for guidance.

Petals Paint Blue Diamond into the upper section of each petal and Amethyst in the lower sections. While paint is still wet, use a pin to streak the colours into each other.

Calyx Use Kelly Green to paint the green base of flower. Comb through with a pin.

Leaves Use Kelly Green for the upper half of each leaf and Emerald Green in the lower half. Comb through with a pin.

Background Paint with Magenta Royale. Comb through with a pin.

Side panels Paint with Royal Blue. Comb through with a pin.

Use a pin to burst any larger air bubbles.
Leave jar lying flat to dry for 12 to 24 hours.
If the jar is to be used and will require washing from time to time, protect the design with a coat of varnish as described on page 18.

SMALL RED DAISY JAR

Illustrated in Figure 17

MATERIALS

small Moccona coffee jar
Plaid Gallery Glass Liquid Leading:
  Soft Black
Plaid Gallery Glass Window Colour:
  Sunny Yellow
  Ruby Red
  White Pearl
  Kelly Green
  Emerald Green
  Ivy Green
  Crystal Clear
3 or 4 plastic grocery bags
toothpick
pin
greaseproof paper

water-based varnish (e.g. Cabot's Crystal Clear)
brush, 12 mm (½ in) flat

METHOD

Trace design onto greaseproof paper and cut out. Insert in jar and pad against surface with crumpled plastic grocery bags.

Lay jar flat to pipe on leading design and allow to dry for approximately 12 to 24 hours.

Apply Window Colour in following sequence, using the photo for guidance.

Flower Use Ruby Red to colour most of each petal, avoiding the inner section. To this area, apply White Pearl and use a pin to comb backwards and forwards to create a streaked effect. Paint centre of flower with Sunny Yellow.

Leaves and stem Use Kelly Green to paint the upper half of the leaf. For stem and lower half of each leaf, use Ivy Green. Comb through with a pin.

Background Use equal amounts of Crystal Clear and Emerald Green in each section, mixed completely together with a toothpick, to create a softer green. Comb through with a pin.

Side panels Paint with Emerald Green. Comb through with a pin.

Use a pin to burst any larger air bubbles. Leave jar lying flat to dry for 12 to 24 hours. If the jar is to be used and will require washing from time to time, protect the design with a coat of varnish as described on page 18.

BLUE FLOWER JAR

Illustrated in Figure 17
MATERIALS
small Moccona coffee jar
Plaid Gallery Glass Liquid Leading:
  Soft Black
Plaid Gallery Glass Window Colour:
  Slate Blue
  White Pearl
  Berry Red
  Blue Diamond
  Kelly Green
  Emerald Green
3 or 4 plastic grocery bags
toothpick
pin
greaseproof paper
water-based varnish (e.g. Cabot's Crystal
  Clear)
brush, 12 mm (½ in) flat

METHOD

Trace design onto greaseproof paper and cut out.

Insert in jar and pad against surface with crumpled plastic grocery bags.

Lay jar flat to pipe on leading design and allow to dry for approximately 12 to 24 hours.

Apply Window Colour in following sequence, using the photo for guidance.

Petals In the upper sections of the three lower petals, squeeze Slate Blue. Paint Blue Diamond over remainder of these petals and use a pin to streak colours together while paint is still wet. The top two petals are painted with Blue Diamond. Comb through with a pin.

Leaves Paint Emerald Green into top section of each leaf and Kelly Green into lower sections. Comb through with a pin.

Background For a soft pink colour, mix equal parts of Berry Red and White Pearl. Combine well in each section using a toothpick, then push to meet edge of leading and comb through with a pin.

Side panels Paint with Slate Blue. Comb through with a pin.

Use a pin to burst any larger air bubbles.
Leave jar lying flat to dry for 12 to 24 hours.
If the jar is to be used and will require washing from time to time, protect the design with a coat of varnish as described on page 18.

SMALL DAFFODIL JAR

Illustrated in Figure 17
MATERIALS
small Moccona coffee jar
Plaid Gallery Glass Liquid Leading:
  Soft Black
Plaid Gallery Glass Window Colour:
  Sunny Yellow
  Royal Blue
  Blue Diamond
  Kelly Green
  Amber
3 or 4 plastic grocery bags
toothpick
pin
greaseproof paper
water-based varnish (e.g. Cabot's Crystal
  Clear)
brush, 12 mm (½ in) flat

METHOD
Trace design onto greaseproof paper and cut out. Insert in jar and pad against surface with crumpled plastic grocery bags.

Lay jar flat to pipe on leading design and allow to dry for approximately 12 to 24 hours.

Apply Window Colour in following sequence, using the photo for guidance.

Flower To give shading to the outer trumpet of the daffodil, apply Amber at the top of this section and Sunny Yellow in remainder of this section. While paint is wet, swirl the two colours together to blend them slightly, using a toothpick.

The remainder of the daffodil is painted with Sunny Yellow. Comb through with a pin.

Stem Paint with Kelly Green. Comb through with a pin.

Background Paint with Blue Diamond. Comb through with a pin.

Side panels Paint with Royal Blue. Comb through with a pin.

Use a pin to burst any larger air bubbles.
Leave jar lying flat to dry for 12 to 24 hours.
If the jar is to be used and will require washing from time to time, protect the design with a coat of varnish as described on page 18.

AUSTRALIAN NATIVE FLOWER CANISTERS

The circular designs painted on these 21 cm (8¼ in) tall canisters, which are available from kitchenware and discount stores, can also be used to make suncatchers, as described on pages 52–57.

If the canisters are intended for decorative purposes only, there will be no need to protect the painted surface. However, if you intend to use them, and will need to wash them from time to time, a coat of varnish will give protection from moisture. Allow the paint to cure for a week. Using a cardboard template with a hole cut out slightly larger than the painted design, lay cardboard over the paintwork and give a light spray of a water-based varnish which is compatible with glass paint.

Do not soak canisters in water, but just wipe over with a soft cloth wrung out in soapy water.

I have created a finer paint finish by warming the tubes in hot (not boiling) water and using a pin to comb through the wet paint. The colours are also softened by mixing with Crystal Clear. You can either combine the colours in each outlined section by swirling together with a toothpick, or mix a larger amount in a tube before you begin painting.

BOTTLEBRUSH CANISTER

Illustrated in Figure 16
MATERIALS
glass canister
Plaid Gallery Glass Liquid Leading:
  Soft Black
Plaid Gallery Glass Window Colour:
  Ruby Red
  Kelly Green
  Denim Blue
  Blue Diamond
  Crystal Clear
Plaid Dimensional Fabric Paint:
  Red Shiny
3 or 4 plastic grocery bags
water-based spray varnish
cardboard
greaseproof paper
pin
toothpick

METHOD
Trace design onto greaseproof paper and cut to size. Insert inside canister and pad with plastic bags to hold design firmly against the surface of the glass and allow you to adjust it to the correct position.

Lay canister on a flat surface and use the Liquid Leading to outline the design. Set aside to dry for 24 hours.

Apply Window Colour paints using the photograph as a guide. Squeeze paint into each section, working one area at a time. Use a toothpick to push paint to touch the edge of leading.

Use a pin to burst any bubbles which appear.

Leave canister lying flat for 24 hours to allow the paint to dry.

Flower Colour with Ruby Red and comb through with a pin.

Leaves and stem Add a little Crystal Clear to Kelly Green to soften colour slightly on upper side of leaf. Use Kelly Green for other side of leaf, stem and tip of flower. Comb through with a pin.

Background Soften background colours by adding an equal amount of Crystal Clear to Blue Diamond, and 2 parts Crystal Clear to 1 part Denim Blue. Comb through with a pin.

Flower stamens When the paint has dried, add the fine detail of long thin stamens with Red Shiny dimensional fabric paint. Where lines overlap, wait for original lines to dry to avoid smudging.

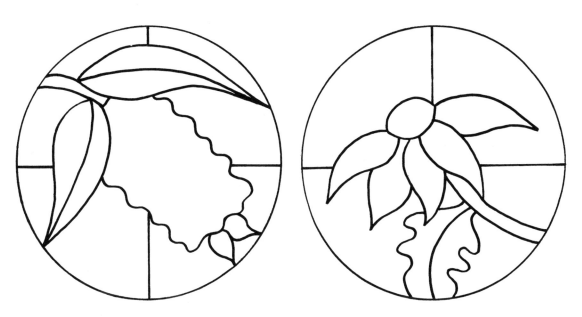

ABOVE: Canister designs: Bottlebrush (page 24), White Flannel Flower (page 27). **ENLARGE AT 185%**

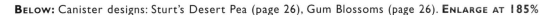

BELOW: Canister designs: Sturt's Desert Pea (page 26), Gum Blossoms (page 26). **ENLARGE AT 185%**

GUM BLOSSOMS CANISTER

Illustrated in Figure 16
MATERIALS
glass canister
Plaid Gallery Glass Liquid Leading:
  Soft Black
Plaid Gallery Glass Window Colour:
  Cocoa Brown
  Orange Poppy
  Ivy Green
  Sunny Yellow
  Amber
  Crystal Clear
Plaid Dimensional Fabric Paint:
  Orange Shiny
3 or 4 plastic grocery bags
water-based spray varnish
cardboard
greaseproof paper
pin
toothpick

METHOD
Trace design onto greaseproof paper and cut to size. Insert inside canister and pad with plastic bags to hold design firmly against the surface of the glass and allow you to adjust it to the correct position.

Lay canister on a flat surface and use the Liquid Leading to outline the design. Set aside to dry for 24 hours.

Apply Window Colour paints using the photograph as a guide. Squeeze paint into each section, working one area at a time. You can use a toothpick to push paint to touch the edge of leading.

Use a pin to burst any bubbles which appear.

Leave canister lying flat for 24 hours to allow the paint to dry.

Flowers Apply Cocoa Brown in top half of gumnut and comb through with a pin. Colour lower section with Orange Poppy and comb through with a pin.

Leaves and stem Soften colour of upper leaf by mixing 2 parts Crystal Clear with 1 part Ivy Green. Comb through with a pin. Use equal amounts of Crystal Clear and Ivy Green for lower leaf sections and stem. Comb through with a pin.

Background Use Sunny Yellow in opposite background areas. Comb through with a pin. Use equal amounts of Crystal Clear and Amber to colour remaining background. Comb through with a pin.

Flower detail When the paint has dried, add the fine detail of the gum blossoms with Orange Shiny dimensional fabric paint.

STURT'S DESERT PEA CANISTER

Illustrated in Figure 16
MATERIALS
glass canister
Plaid Gallery Glass Liquid Leading:
  Soft Black

Plaid Gallery Glass Window Colour:
  Ruby Red
  Emerald Green
  Ivy Green
  Kelly Green

FIGURE 9: Laying down a dry leading strip

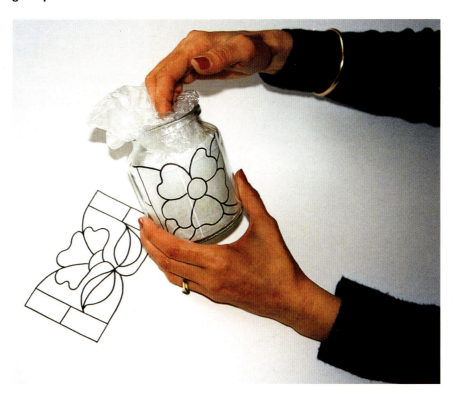

FIGURE 10: Padding a coffee jar
with plastic grocery bags to
keep the traced design in place

Figure 13: Blending cheek colour with a pin

Figure 14: The criss-cross technique of applying background colour

FIGURE 15: Vases with
cheerful flower designs
(see pages 12–17)

FIGURE 16: A set of canisters decorated with
Australian native flowers
(see pages 24–28)

FIGURE 17: Coffee jars large and small can be merely decorative, but can also be used if the designs are protected with a coat of varnish (see pages 18–23)

FIGURE 18: Mermaid and dolphins in a découpaged frame (see pages 29–31)

FIGURE 19: Underwater subjects lend themselves to glass painting (see pages 31–33)

FIGURE 20: You may prefer to work these cheerful Beach People as three separate frames (see pages 39–43)

FIGURE 21: Iris frame
(see pages 35–36)

FIGURE 22: Tulip frame
(see pages 35–37)

FIGURE 23: Poppy frame (see pages 36–38)

FIGURE 24: Sunflower frame (see pages 36–38)

FIGURE 25: This Pear and Cherry design would brighten up a kitchen window (see pages 32–34)

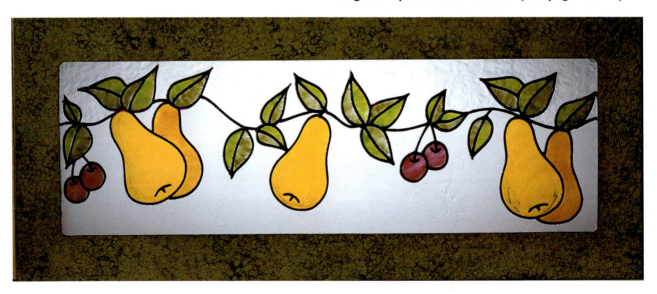

Crystal Clear
Plaid Dimensional Fabric Paint:
  Black Shiny
3 or 4 plastic grocery bags
water-based spray varnish
cardboard
greaseproof paper
pin
toothpick

METHOD

Trace design onto greaseproof paper and cut to size. Insert inside canister and pad with plastic bags to hold design firmly against the surface of the glass and allow you to adjust it to the correct position.

Lay canister on a flat surface and use the Liquid Leading to outline the design. Set aside to dry for 24 hours.

Apply Window Colour paints using the photograph as a guide. Squeeze paint into each section, working one area at a time. Use a toothpick to push paint to touch the edge of leading.

Use a pin to burst any bubbles which appear.

Leave canister lying flat for 24 hours to allow the paint to dry.

Flower Use Ruby Red to colour flower petals and comb through with a pin.

Leaves Colour with Emerald Green and comb through with a pin.

Background Colour top left and lower right with a mix of equal amounts of Crystal Clear and Ivy Green. Colour remaining background with a mix of equal amounts of Crystal Clear and Kelly Green. Comb through with a pin.

Flower centres When the paint has dried, fill in the centres of the Sturt's desert pea flowers with the Black Shiny dimensional fabric paint. If you prefer to use only glass paint in your work, you can fill in the centres using the leading. Allow to dry for another 24 hours.

WHITE FLANNEL FLOWER CANISTER

Illustrated in Figure 16
MATERIALS
glass canister
Plaid Gallery Glass Liquid Leading:
  Soft Black
Plaid Gallery Glass Window Colour:
  Snow White
  Sunny Yellow
  Emerald Green
  Kelly Green
  Blue Diamond
  Denim Blue
  Crystal Clear
Plaid Dimensional Fabric Paint:
  Yellow Pearl
3 or 4 plastic grocery bags

water-based spray varnish
cardboard
greaseproof paper
pin
toothpick

METHOD

Trace design onto greaseproof paper and cut to size. Insert inside canister and pad with plastic bags to hold design firmly against the surface of the glass and allow you to adjust it to the correct position.

Lay canister on a flat surface and use the Liquid Leading to outline the design. Set aside to dry for 24 hours.

Apply Window Colour paints using the photograph as a guide. Squeeze paint into each section, working one area at a time. You can use a toothpick to push paint to touch the edge of leading.

Use a pin to burst any bubbles which appear.

Leave canister lying flat for 24 hours to allow the paint to dry.

Flower Apply Sunny Yellow to centre and comb through with a pin.

Colour petals in Snow White and comb through with a pin.

Leaf and stem Use Emerald Green with a touch of Crystal Clear to colour left side of leaf. Comb through with a pin. For other side of leaf, and for stem, use an equal mix of Crystal Clear and Kelly Green. Comb through with a pin.

Background Soften background colours by adding an equal amount of Crystal Clear to Blue Diamond, and 2 parts Crystal Clear to 1 part Denim Blue. Comb through with a pin.

Flower detail When the paint has dried, add dots of Yellow Pearl dimensional fabric paint at the base of centre for more interest. Allow to dry for another 24 hours.

FRIEZE FRAMES

These friezes can be made up as individual frames to be hung as a decoration. Each design can also be adapted for use as a border for a window or a mirror.

MERMAID FRAME

Illustrated in Figure 18
On the frame surrounding this design I have découpaged coordinating mermaids from a découpage paper distributed by Finmark Découpage, paper code JE209. For international distributors, check Web Site www.chariot.net.au./~finmark or fax 61 (0) 8 82770662

MATERIALS
frame with clip-in glass, approx. 42 x 72 cm (16½ x 28½ in)
Plaid Gallery Glass Liquid Leading:
  Soft Black
Plaid Gallery Glass Window Colour:
  Crystal Clear
  Sunny Yellow
  Amber
  Canyon Coral
  Ruby Red
  Royal Blue
  Emerald Green
  Turquoise
  White Pearl
  Blue Diamond
toothpicks
pin

METHOD
If necessary, enlarge the design to fit your frame.

Remove glass from frame and lay over the top of design. Use Liquid Leading to outline the designs and set aside to dry until firm to touch.

Apply Window Colours in the following order, following the photograph for guidance.

TIPS To make the fine lines for the eyes and mouth, use a sticky tape extension, as described on page 4, to make the nozzle finer. Pull the sides of the mouth out with a pin while leading is still wet. Pipe the scales on the mermaid's tail *after* the colour has been applied and dried out, as it would be difficult to blend the colours with this fine detail already in place.

Mermaid's skin Use Canyon Coral to colour all skin areas. While paint is wet, pick up a tiny dot of Ruby Red on the tip of a pin and blend in a small circle to create rosy cheeks. Comb through other skin areas to distribute the paint more evenly and achieve an even colour when dry.

Mermaid's tail Apply Royal Blue in the upper area of tail and Emerald Green to the lower tail area. While paint is still wet, blend to merge colours, using a toothpick. Run the toothpick backwards and forwards through the wet paint to create a soft transition of colour.

Hair and starfish Use Amber and Sunny Yellow to colour these areas, referring to the photo for colour placement.

Frieze Frame design:
Mermaid (page 29).
Enlarge at 342%

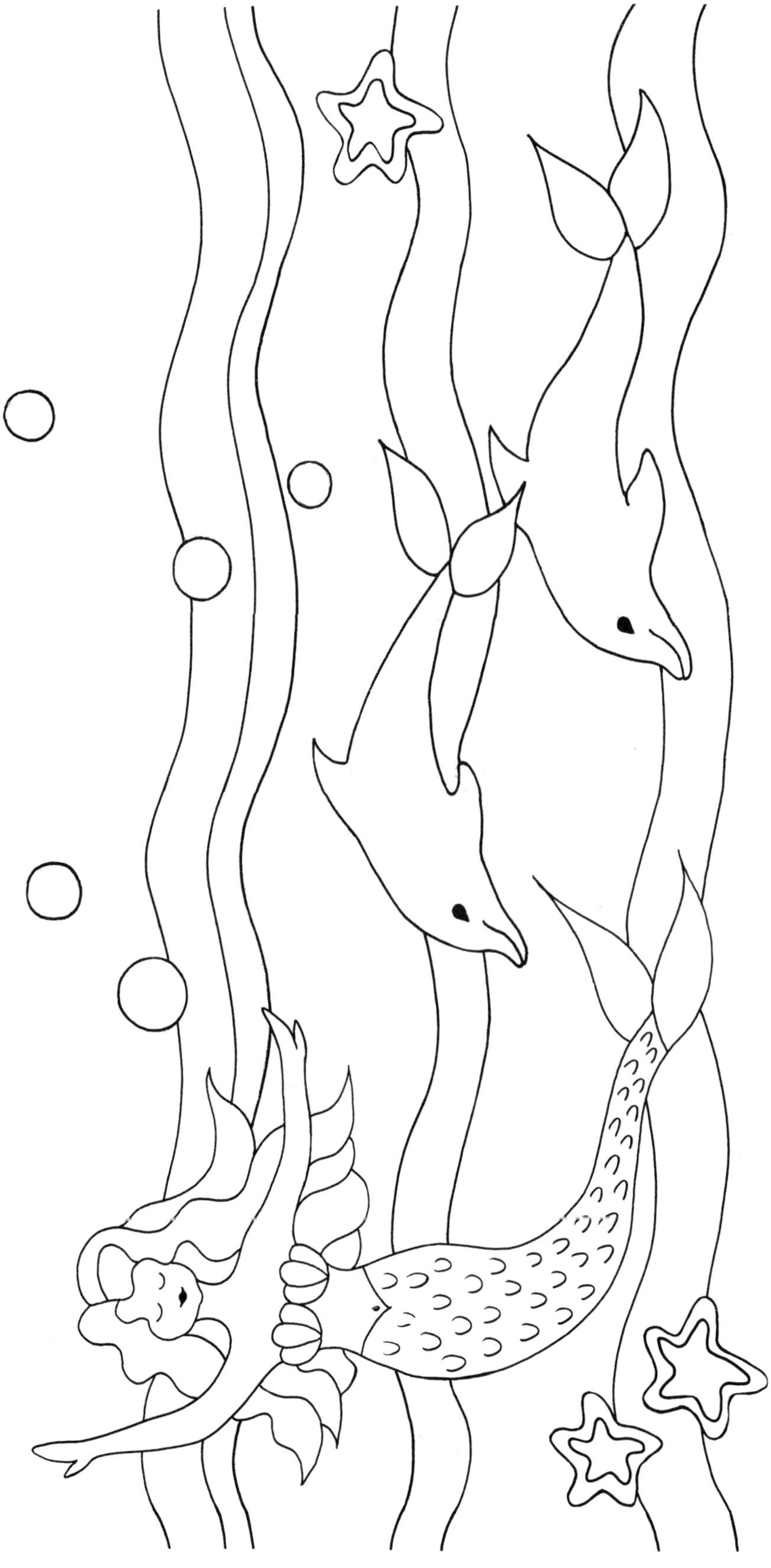

Dolphins Paint each dolphin's body all over with Royal Blue. While paint is wet, apply a thin band of White Pearl along underbelly. Use a toothpick to blend the wet paints together, working with a short backwards and forwards motion so you do not spread the White Pearl too much.

Bubbles Paint all bubbles with White Pearl.

Waves Referring to photo for correct colour placement, alternate between Turquoise and Blue Diamond. When combing through the wet paint, follow the line of the leading.

Clear background Apply Crystal Clear to background area and while it is still wet swirl a toothpick through the paint to create a textured finish.

Use a pin to burst any air bubbles which may appear.

Leave paint to dry completely, and then use Liquid Leading to pipe in the scales on the mermaid's tail, making the nozzle finer with sticky tape. Allow to dry.

When all paint and leading has dried, clip glass back into frame.

LARGE FISH FRAME

Illustrated in Figure 19
MATERIALS
frame with clip-in glass, approx. 60 x 20 cm
  (23½ x 8 in)
Plaid Gallery Glass Liquid Leading:
  Soft Black
Plaid Gallery Glass Window Colour:
  Crystal Clear
  Snow White
  Emerald Green
  Sunny Yellow
  Amber
  Blue Diamond
  Royal Blue
  Slate Blue
  Denim Blue
toothpick
pin

METHOD
If you are working this design onto an existing upright window, follow the method for vertical application described on pages 9–10.

To work the design on framed glass, remove glass from frame and work directly onto glass surface in the usual manner. Outline the design in Liquid Leading and set aside to dry until the leading is firm to touch, approximately 12 to 24 hours.

Apply Window Colour in the following sequence, referring to the photograph for guidance.

Two-tone blue fish Squeeze Blue Diamond in upper section of body. Apply Denim Blue in lower body area and use a toothpick in a backwards and forwards action to blend the two colours together slightly. Make sure the paint reaches the edge of leading.

While paint is still wet in the body of fish, draw in scales using Slate Blue. This will give a slightly muted effect when the two wet paints settle together.

Colour the fins in Blue Diamond, and the tail in alternate stripes of Slate Blue and Blue Diamond.

At the upper and lower tips of the tail I have added a small amount of Snow White and streaked it into either colour, using a toothpick to blend the paint.

Blue and green fish Squeeze Blue Diamond in upper body and Royal Blue in lower section.

ABOVE: Frieze Frame designs: Large Fish (page 31). **ENLARGE AT 298%**
BELOW: Frieze Frame design: Pear and Cherry (page 33). **ENLARGE AT 298%**

While the paints are still wet, streak them together slightly using a toothpick. Make sure that the paint touches the leading to avoid any light holes in your work. While paint is still wet in body section, use Emerald Green to draw in scales.

Paint both fins with Royal Blue, and the tail with alternate stripes of Emerald Green and Royal Blue. As with the first fish, at the upper and lower tips of the tail I have added a small amount of Snow White and streaked it into either colour, using a toothpick to blend the paint.

Yellow shell At the base of shell, apply Amber and comb through to meet the edge of the leading. Squeeze a small amount of Amber in lower main section and use Sunny Yellow to colour the remainder of the shell. Use a toothpick to streak these colours together slightly.

Along upper curve of shell, squeeze large dots of Snow White over the top of the Sunny Yellow while the paint is still wet.

Striped shell Use alternate stripes of Sunny Yellow and Slate Blue to colour this shell.

White shell Use Snow White to colour all of this shell except for the 'opening' in the lower section. Colour this with Slate Blue. Squeeze small dots of Slate Blue over the top of the Snow White while the paint is wet, following the photo for colour placement.

Reeds The darker reeds are coloured with Emerald Green. The lighter green reeds are coloured with a mix of 3 parts Snow White and 1 part Emerald Green. Squeeze the two colours into each outlined area and mix well with a toothpick to combine colour, then push the paint to meet the edges of the leading. Comb through paint to distribute colour evenly.

Bubbles Colour these with Snow White.

Background Use Crystal Clear to colour in the background, creating a texture in the paint by using a toothpick to draw figure eights through the wet paint. Once the paint is dry, the texture will be more obvious.

Prick any air bubbles with a pin and leave to dry for 24 to 48 hours.

Clip glass back into frame.

PEAR AND CHERRY FRAME

Illustrated in Figure 25
MATERIALS
frame with clip-in glass, approx. 60 x 20 cm
  (23½ x 8 in)
Plaid Gallery Glass Liquid Leading:
  Soft Black
Plaid Gallery Glass Window Colour:
  Crystal Clear
  Clear Frost
  Sunny Yellow
  Kelly Green
  Amber
  Berry Red

  Ivy Green
toothpicks
pin
flat paintbrush, 12 mm (½ in)

METHOD
If you are working this design onto an existing upright window, follow the method for vertical application described on pages 9–10.

To work the design on framed glass, remove glass from frame and work directly onto glass surface in the usual manner. Outline the design in Liquid Leading and set aside to dry until the leading is firm to touch, approximately 12 to 24 hours.

Apply Window Colour following this sequence, and referring to the photograph for guidance.

Pears Use Sunny Yellow for the three foreground pears. Spread paint to meet the edges of the leading and comb through to distribute evenly. While paint is still wet, squeeze a few dots of Kelly Green on the fat lower part of each pear and use a toothpick to streak into Sunny Yellow.

For the two pears in the background, use a mixture of 2 parts Amber and 1 part Sunny Yellow. Mix colours well together and push with toothpick to meet the edges of the leading. Comb through to distribute paint evenly.

Cherries Colour cherries with Berry Red.

Leaves Each leaf is two-tone, with Kelly Green on one half and Ivy Green on the other. Refer to photo for colour placement. The brighter green is Kelly Green.

Background In the upper part of the background I have used Crystal Clear. Apply paint to background and push to meet the edges of the leading with a toothpick. Create a texture in this paint by using a toothpick to swirl or draw figure eights when the paint is still wet. When this dries, it creates an interesting contrast to the lower Clear Frost section.

In the lower background area apply Clear Frost in the following way: squeeze Clear Frost onto a palette (tile or plastic lid) and use the paintbrush to apply paint. Pick up some paint on brush and apply with overlapping crisscross strokes until entire background is covered. Make sure Clear Frost covers leading. Do not worry if paint goes onto any coloured area slightly, as when paint dries it will not be noticeable.

TIP The crisscross method is an extremely quick method of applying a background.

Use a pin to burst any large air bubbles.

Set the finished work aside to dry for 24 to 48 hours and then clip glass back into frame.

FLOWER FRAMES

IRIS FRAME

Illustrated in Figure 21
MATERIALS
frame with clip-in glass, approx. 25 x 19 cm
(10 x 7½ in)
Plaid Gallery Glass Liquid Leading:
Soft Black
Plaid Gallery Glass Window Colour:
Crystal Clear
Sunny Yellow
Kelly Green
Ivy Green
Amethyst
Royal Blue
toothpicks
pin

METHOD
Remove glass from frame to decorate and place design underneath.

Use Liquid Leading to outline the design and set aside to dry for approximately 24 hours.

Referring to photo for colour placement and working each outlined section individually, apply Window Colour in the following sequence.

Petals Leaving an area free of paint in the centre of the main lower petal, apply Amethyst over the outer areas of each petal. Squeeze Royal Blue onto the inner section of each petal. While both paints are wet, spread each colour to meet the edge of the leading, then use a toothpick to comb through both colours to blend together. Make sure paint is distributed evenly.

Squeeze Sunny Yellow into the area you have left free of colour on the main lower petal. Do not streak any of the yellow into the other paint, as a more solid colour is required.

Leaves and stems Following the photo for colour placement, paint the leaves with Kelly Green (the brighter green) and Ivy Green. Paint the longer stem in Ivy Green and the short stem in Kelly Green.

Background The centre diamond is left free of paint. On the four triangular corners, spread Crystal Clear to meet the edges of the leading and then swirl through wet paint with a toothpick to create a texture.

Use a pin to burst any larger air bubbles.

Leave in a horizontal position to dry for 24 to 48 hours, before clipping glass back into frame.

TULIP FRAME

Illustrated in Figure 22
MATERIALS
frame with clip-in glass, approx. 25 x 19 cm
(10 x 7½ in)
Plaid Gallery Glass Liquid Leading:
Soft Black
Plaid Gallery Glass Window Colour:
Crystal Clear

ABOVE: Flower Frame designs: Iris (page 35), Tulip (page 35). **ENLARGE AT 233%**
BELOW: Flower Frame designs: Poppy (page 37), Sunflower (page 38). **ENLARGE AT 233%**

Sunny Yellow
Amber
Kelly Green
Emerald Green
toothpicks
pin

METHOD

Remove glass from frame to decorate and place design underneath.

Use Liquid Leading to outline the design and set aside to dry for approximately 24 hours.

Referring to photo for colour placement and working each outlined section individually, apply Window Colour in the following sequence.

Petals Apply Sunny Yellow only in upper section of petal.

Apply Sunny Yellow to the outside of the petals, adding a little Amber at the base and top of the petals. While paint is still wet, use a toothpick to streak paint together.

Leaves and stems All leaves are painted in Kelly Green, with the exception of the curled-back leaf on left-hand side which is painted in Emerald Green. Paint the three stems in Emerald Green.

Background The centre diamond is left free of paint. On the four triangular corners use Crystal Clear. Spread the paint to meet the edges of the leading and then swirl through wet paint with a toothpick to create a texture.

Use a pin to burst any larger air bubbles.

Leave in a horizontal position to dry for 24 to 48 hours before clipping glass back into frame.

POPPY FRAME

Illustrated in Figure 23
MATERIALS
frame with clip-in glass, approx. 25 x 19 cm
  (10 x 7½ in)
Plaid Gallery Glass Liquid Leading:
  Soft Black
Plaid Gallery Glass Window Colour:
  Crystal Clear
  Ruby Red
  White Pearl
  Kelly Green
  Ivy Green
toothpicks
pin

METHOD

Remove glass from frame to decorate and place design underneath.

Use Liquid Leading to outline the design and set aside to dry for approximately 24 hours.

Referring to Figure 23 for colour placement and working on each outlined section individually, apply Window Colour in the following sequence.

Petals Paint the three back petals of each flower, and tip of bud, with Ruby Red. Apply a strip of White Pearl along the upper part of the front petal of each flower, and apply Ruby Red over the remainder of petal. While the paints are still wet, use a toothpick to blend well into each other so the upper area appears lighter in colour. Comb through the paint to distribute evenly.

Leaves and stems Use Kelly Green to colour the leaf on the left-hand side. Use Ivy Green for the leaf behind stem. The bud and stems are coloured Kelly Green.

Background The centre diamond is left free of paint. Use Crystal Clear on the four triangular corners. Spread the paint to meet the edge of the leading and then swirl through wet paint with a toothpick to create a texture.

Use a pin to burst any larger air bubbles.

Leave in a horizontal position to dry, before clipping glass back into frame.

SUNFLOWER FRAME

Illustrated in Figure 24

MATERIALS
Frame with clip in glass, approx 25x19 cm
 (10in x 7½ in)
Plaid Gallery Glass Liquid Leading
 Soft Black
Plaid Gallery Glass Window Colour
 Crystal Clear
 Sunny Yellow
 Amber
 Cocoa Brown
 Kelly Green
 Ivy Green
Toothpicks
Pin
Paper towel

METHOD
Remove glass from frame and place design underneath.

Use Liquid Leading to outline the design and set aside to dry for approximately 24 hours (do not apply lead in shaded area of flower centre).

Working each outlined section individually, apply Window Colour in following sequence.

Sunflower Petals Paint the petals in Sunny Yellow, blending a little Amber into Sunny Yellow where petals join flower centre. Also blend amber into Sunny Yellow on background petals to create the effect of shading.

Flower Centres Use Cocoa Brown to colour complete centre and comb through with a toothpick. Refer to design: to deepen the middle area of centre, add a small swirl of Liquid Leading over wet paint and use a toothpick to swirl paint and leading together to create a darker brown circle in the middle of flower centre. Use the tip of toothpick to create a dotted texture over entire centre.

Leaves and stems Use Ivy Green to paint the lower section of each leaf and Kelly Green for the upper leaf area. Paint the long stem in Kelly Green and the two shorter stems in Ivy Green.

Background The centre diamond is left free of paint.

On the four triangular corners use Crystal Clear. Spread the paint to meet the edges of the leading and then swirl though wet paint with a toothpick to create a texture.

Use a pin to burst any larger air bubbles.

Leave in horizontal position to dry for 24 to 48 hours before clipping glass back into frame.

BEACH PEOPLE

The three parts of this design can either be used separately or combined in a longer frame, as shown in Figure 20. The design will also adapt as a window border on an existing upright window. For the combined picture you will need a long frame, approximately 21 x 51 cm (8¼ x 20 in); for individual pictures you will need frames approximately 21 x 17 cm (8¼ x 6½ in).

MAN IN STRIPED BATHERS

Illustrated in Figure 20
MATERIALS
frame with clip-in glass approx. 21 x 17 cm
  (8¼ x 6½ in)
Plaid Gallery Glass Liquid Leading:
  Soft Black
Plaid Gallery Glass Window Colour:
  Crystal Clear
  Sunny Yellow
  Canyon Coral
  Royal Blue
  Ruby Red
  Amber
  White Pearl
toothpicks
pin

METHOD
Remove glass from frame to decorate and place design underneath.

Use Liquid Leading to outline the design and set aside to dry for approximately 24 hours.

Referring to photo for colour placement and working each outlined section individually, apply Window Colour in the following sequence.

Skin and hair Colour all skin areas with Canyon Coral and comb through with toothpick to distribute the colour evenly. Colour hair and moustache with Sunny Yellow.

Bathers Paint alternate stripes in White Pearl and Ruby Red.

Ice-cream Use Amber to colour the cone and White Pearl for ice-cream.

Sun Use Sunny Yellow for the central area of the sun. Use Sunny Yellow plus Amber for the spikes around the sun. Blend colours together with a toothpick.

Water For the lighter blue areas of water use mixed White Pearl and Royal Blue. Add equal amounts of the two colours in each outlined section and blend well together with a toothpick before pushing out to meet edges of the leading. Darker blue water is Royal Blue. Comb through following the line of water.

Background Sky area is Crystal Clear. Spread to meet edges of leading and, while paint is still wet, use toothpick to swirl through paint to create a texture.

Use a pin to prick any air bubbles if necessary.

Set aside to dry for 24 to 48 hours and clip glass back into frame.

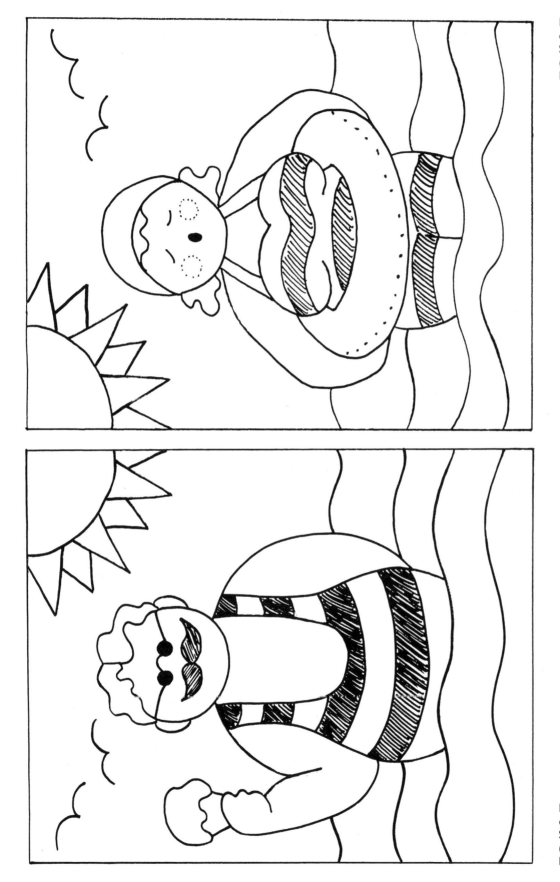

LEFT: Beach People designs: Man In Striped Bathers (page 39).
ENLARGE AT 154%

LEFT: Beach People designs: Woman In Striped Bathers (page 41).
ENLARGE AT 154%

WOMAN IN STRIPED BATHERS

Illustrated in Figure 20
MATERIALS
frame with clip-in glass approx. 21 x 17 cm
(8¼ x 6½ in)
Plaid Gallery Glass Liquid Leading:
  Soft Black
Plaid Gallery Glass Window Colour:
  Crystal Clear
  Sunny Yellow
  Canyon Coral
  Royal Blue
  Ruby Red
  Amber
  White Pearl
  Emerald Green
toothpicks
pin

METHOD
Remove glass from frame to decorate and place design underneath.

Use Liquid Leading to outline the design and set aside to dry for approximately 24 hours.

Referring to photo for colour placement and working each outlined section individually, apply Window Colour in the following sequence.

Skin and hair Colour all skin areas with Canyon Coral and comb through with toothpick to distribute the colour evenly. While Canyon Coral is still wet, pick up a tiny dot of Ruby Red on the tip of a pin and swirl in a circle in cheek area to blend into rosy cheeks. Paint hair with Amber.

Life-belt Colour with White Pearl. Try to avoid covering the dots of leading, although when the paint dries transparent they will still be noticeable.

Bathers Paint in alternate stripes of Emerald Green and Sunny Yellow.

Bathing hat Paint with Emerald Green.

Sun Use Sunny Yellow to colour central area of sun. Use Sunny Yellow plus Amber for the spikes around sun. Blend colours together with a toothpick.

Water For the lighter blue areas of water use mixed White Pearl and Royal Blue. Add equal amounts of the two colours in each outlined section and blend well together with a toothpick before pushing out to meet edges of the leading. Darker blue water is Royal Blue. Comb through following the line of water.

Background Sky area is Crystal Clear. Spread to meet edges of leading and while paint is still wet, use toothpick to swirl through paint to create a texture.

Use a pin to prick any air bubbles if necessary.

Set aside to dry for 24 to 48 hours and clip glass back into frame.

WOMAN WITH BEACHBALL

Illustrated in Figure 20
MATERIALS
frame with clip-in glass approx. 21 x 17 cm
  (8¼ x 6½ in)
Plaid Gallery Glass Liquid Leading:
  Soft Black
Plaid Gallery Glass Window Colour:
  Crystal Clear
  Sunny Yellow
  Canyon Coral
  Royal Blue
  Ruby Red
  White Pearl
toothpicks
pin

METHOD
Remove glass from frame to decorate and place design underneath.

Use Liquid Leading to outline the design and set aside to dry for approximately 24 hours.

Referring to photo for colour placement and working each outlined section individually, apply Window Colour in the following sequence.

Skin and hair Colour all skin areas with Canyon Coral and comb through with toothpick to distribute the colour evenly. While Canyon Coral is still wet, pick up a tiny dot of Ruby Red on the tip of a pin and swirl in a circle in cheek area to blend into rosy cheeks. Colour hair with Sunny Yellow.

Bathers Use Ruby Red to colour all of bathers area. Wait for the paint to semi-set before adding spots of White Pearl. This will ensure the spots won't blend into Ruby Red paint.

Bathing hat Colour with Ruby Red.

Beachball Use Royal Blue and White Pearl.

Water For the lighter blue areas of water use mixed White Pearl and Royal Blue. Add equal amounts of the two colours in each outlined section and blend well together with a toothpick before pushing out to meet edges of the leading. Darker blue water is Royal Blue. Comb through following the line of water.

Fish Colour with White Pearl.

Background Sky area is Crystal Clear. Spread to meet edges of leading and while paint is still wet, use toothpick to swirl through paint to create a texture.

Use a pin to prick any air bubbles if necessary.

Set aside to dry for 24 to 48 hours and clip glass back into frame. Use a pin to prick any air bubbles if necessary.

FIGURE 26: The pear and lemon designs are part of the set of Small Fruit Frames (see pages 44–46)

FIGURE 27: Cherries and plums make up the remainder of the set of Small Fruit Frames from pages 46–47

Snail design
(see pages 48–49

Ladybug
design (see
pages 49–50)

Butterfly design
(see pages 48–49

Moon design (see pages 49–50)

Sun design
(see pages
49–51)

FIGURE 28: Peel and Press designs

FIGURE 29: Suncatcher design for Yellow Fish (see pages 52–53)

FIGURE 30: Suncatcher design for Striped Fish (see pages 53–54)

FIGURE 31: Suncatcher design for
White Daisy (see pages 53–54)

FIGURE 32: Suncatcher design for
Orange Tiger Lily (see pages 53, 55)

FIGURE 33:
Suncatcher design
for Full Butterfly
(see pages 55–57)

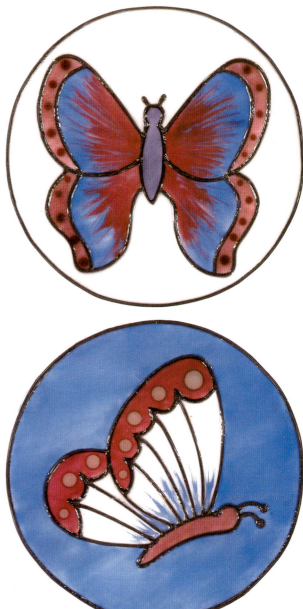

FIGURE 34: Suncatcher design for
Half Butterfly (see pages 56–57)

ABOVE: Beach People designs: Woman With Beachball (page 42). **ACTUAL SIZE**

SMALL FRUIT FRAMES

I have created tartan frames to complement the colours in the paintings. Wooden frames were basecoated yellow, and stripes of colour painted over when dry. I used a gold foil finish for the overlying stripes.

PEAR FRAME

Illustrated in Figure 26
MATERIALS
frame with clip-in glass approx. 13 cm (5 in)
  square
Plaid Gallery Glass Liquid Leading:
  Soft Black
Plaid Gallery Glass Window Colour:
  Crystal Clear
  Amber
  Kelly Green
  Emerald Green
  Sunny Yellow
toothpicks
pin

METHOD
Remove glass from frame to decorate and place design underneath.

Use Liquid Leading to outline the design and set aside to dry for approximately 24 hours.

Referring to photo for colour placement and working each outlined section individually, apply Window Colour in the following sequence.

Pear Use Sunny Yellow to colour all of the pear. Push paint to meet edge of leading. While paint is still wet, streak a small amount of Kelly Green in the lower half of pear. Make sure green is blended in softly to create interest, rather than solid stripes.

Leaves and stalk Use Kelly Green to colour stalk and upper half of each leaf. Colour lower leaf section in Emerald Green.

Background Paint Amber into opposite corners (refer to photo). Make sure paint touches the edge of leading and comb through to distribute colour evenly.

Use Crystal Clear on the other two background squares. Swirl toothpick through wet Crystal Clear paint to create a texture.

Use a pin to burst any air bubbles and allow project to dry for 24 to 48 hours.

Once dry, clip glass back into frame.

LEMON FRAME

Illustrated in Figure 26
MATERIALS
frame with clip-in glass approx. 13 cm (5 in)
  square

Plaid Gallery Glass Liquid Leading:
  Soft Black
Plaid Gallery Glass Window Colour:
  Crystal Clear

Above: Small Fruit Frame designs: Pear (page 44), Lemon (page 46). **Enlarge at 161%**

Below: Small Fruit Frame designs: Cherry (page 46), Plum (page 47). **Enlarge at 161%**

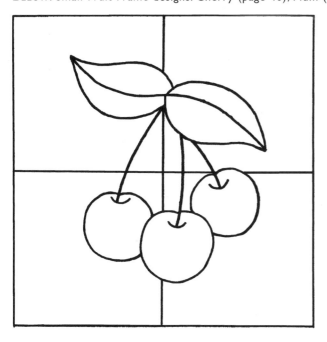

Royal Blue
Kelly Green
Emerald Green
Sunny Yellow
toothpicks
pin

METHOD

Remove glass from frame to decorate and place design underneath.

Use Liquid Leading to outline the design and set aside to dry for approximately 24 hours.

Referring to photo for colour placement and working each outlined section individually, apply Window Colour in the following sequence.

Lemon Use Sunny Yellow to colour all of lemon. Push paint to meet the edge of leading then comb through wet paint to distribute colour evenly.

While paint is wet, swirl a dot of Kelly Green (pick up on the end of a toothpick) in lower section of lemon.

Leaves and stalk Use Kelly Green to colour stalk and upper half of each leaf. Colour lower leaf section in Emerald Green.

Background Paint Royal Blue in opposite corners. Comb through paint to distribute colour, making sure paint touches the edge of leading.

Use Crystal Clear on the other two background squares. Swirl toothpick through wet Crystal Clear paint to create a texture.

Use a pin to burst any air bubbles and allow project to dry for 24 to 48 hours.

Once dry, clip glass back into frame.

CHERRY FRAME

Illustrated in Figure 27
MATERIALS
frame with clip-in glass approx. 13 cm (5 in)
  square
Plaid Gallery Glass Liquid Leading:
  Soft Black
Plaid Gallery Glass Window Colour:
  Crystal Clear
  Berry Red
  Kelly Green
  Emerald Green
  Sunny Yellow
toothpicks
pin

METHOD

Remove glass from frame to decorate and place design underneath.

Use Liquid Leading to outline the design and set aside to dry for approximately 24 hours.

Referring to photo for colour placement and working each outlined section individually, apply Window Colour in the following sequence.

Cherries Use Berry Red to colour the two outer cherries. Use a mix of Crystal Clear and Berry Red on the middle cherry to make it slightly lighter in colour. Push paint to meet the edge of leading then comb through wet paint to distribute colour evenly.

Leaves Use Kelly Green to colour upper half of each leaf. Colour lower leaf section in Emerald Green.

Background Paint Sunny Yellow in opposite corners. Comb through paint to distribute colour, making sure paint touches the edge of leading.

Use Crystal Clear on the other two background squares. Swirl toothpick through wet Crystal Clear paint to create a texture.

Use a pin to burst any air bubbles and allow project to dry for 24 to 48 hours.

Once dry, clip glass back into frame.

PLUM FRAME

Illustrated in Figure 27
MATERIALS
frame with clip-in glass approx. 13 cm (5 in)
  square
Plaid Gallery Glass Liquid Leading:
  Soft Black
Plaid Gallery Glass Window Colour:
  Crystal Clear
  Magenta
  Kelly Green
  Emerald Green
toothpicks
pin

METHOD
Remove glass from frame to decorate and place design underneath.

Use Liquid Leading to outline the design and set aside to dry for approximately 24 hours.

Referring to photo for colour placement and working each outlined section individually, apply Window Colour in the following sequence.

Plums Use Magenta to colour plums. Push paint to meet the edge of leading then comb through wet paint to distribute colour evenly.

Leaves and stalk Use Kelly Green to colour upper half of each leaf. Colour lower leaf section and stalk in Emerald Green.

Background The soft green background squares are a mix of 1 part Emerald Green and 2 parts Crystal Clear. Mix the two colours together in the middle of each square then use a toothpick to push paint to meet edge of leading. Comb through wet paint to distribute colour evenly.

Use Crystal Clear on the other two background squares. Swirl toothpick through wet Crystal Clear paint to create a texture.

Use a pin to burst any air bubbles and allow project to dry for 24 to 48 hours.

Once dry, clip glass back into frame.

PEEL AND PRESS DESIGNS

You can create individual designs to attach to mirrors, windows or tiles. This group of fun designs will undoubtedly appeal to children.

All you require are an A4 plastic sleeve, Plaid Liquid Leading and Plaid Window Colour.

Individual elements of many of the designs in this book can be used in this way, instead of working a complete picture. Just use your imagination to brighten any room.

SNAIL

Illustrated in Figure 28
MATERIALS
Plaid Gallery Glass Liquid Leading:
  Soft Black
Plaid Gallery Glass Window Colour:
  White Pearl
  Emerald Green
  Sunny Yellow
plastic A4 sleeve
toothpicks
pin

METHOD
Insert design inside plastic sleeve and outline in Liquid Leading. Allow to dry overnight or until the leading is firm to the touch, then apply Window Colour in the following sequence.

Body Use White Pearl for snail's body.

Shell Apply Emerald Green over shell with a touch of Sunny Yellow in places. Use your toothpick to swirl through these two colours, but do not mix completely. This will give a more interesting effect when dry.

Use a pin to burst any air bubbles.

Set aside to dry for 24 to 48 hours. When completely dry, gently peel the snail off the plastic and attach it to a clean glass or tile surface, pressing from the top downwards, applying firm pressure to remove any air from underneath. It will remain firmly fixed if left undisturbed.

BUTTERFLY

Illustrated in Figure 28
MATERIALS
Plaid Gallery Glass Liquid Leading:
  Soft Black
Plaid Gallery Glass Window Colour:
  Berry Red
  Royal Blue
  White Pearl
  Amethyst
plastic A4 sleeve
toothpicks
pin

METHOD
Insert design inside plastic sleeve and outline in Liquid Leading. Allow to dry overnight or until

ABOVE: Peel and Press designs: Snail (page 48). **ACTUAL SIZE**

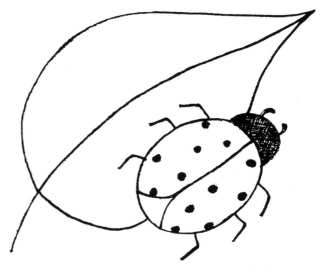

ABOVE: Peel and Press designs: Ladybug (page 50). **ENLARGE AT 133%**

ABOVE: Peel and Press designs: Sun (page 51). **ACTUAL SIZE**

ABOVE: Peel and Press designs: Butterfly (page 48). **ACTUAL SIZE**

LEFT: Peel and Press designs: Moon (page 51). **ACTUAL SIZE**

the leading is firm to the touch, then apply Window Colour in the following sequence.

Body Colour body with Berry Red.

Wings Squeeze a line of Amethyst along inside edge of wing, then use White Pearl to colour remainder of inner wing section. Use a toothpick to streak Amethyst into White Pearl, moving toothpick backwards and forwards.

Outer wing area is coloured with Royal Blue.

While paint is still wet, squeeze different sized spots of White Pearl over the Royal Blue.

Use a pin to burst any air bubbles.

Set aside to dry for 24 to 48 hours. When completely dry gently peel the butterfly off the plastic and attach it to a clean glass or tile surface, pressing from the top downwards, applying firm pressure to remove any air from underneath. It will remain firmly fixed if left undisturbed.

LADYBUG

Illustrated in Figure 28
MATERIALS
Plaid Gallery Glass Liquid Leading:
  Soft Black
Plaid Gallery Glass Window Colour:
  Ruby Red
  Kelly Green
  Emerald Green
plastic A4 sleeve
toothpicks
pin

METHOD
Insert design inside plastic sleeve and outline in Liquid Leading. Do not apply dots of leading on ladybug's wings at this stage, as this will be easier to add over the top of dry Ruby Red Window Colour paint. Allow to dry overnight or until the leading is firm to the touch, then apply Window Colour in the following sequence.

Leaf Colour left side of leaf with Emerald Green. Use Kelly Green for the other half of the leaf. Comb through with a toothpick and use opposite greens to draw vein lines over wet paint.

Head Fill in head area with Liquid Leading.

Wings Colour wings with Ruby Red and, when dry, squeeze dots of leading over the top.

Use a pin to burst any air bubbles.

Set aside to dry for 24 to 48 hours. When completely dry, gently peel the ladybug off the plastic and attach it to a clean glass or tile surface, pressing from the top downwards, applying firm pressure to remove any air from underneath. It will remain firmly fixed if left undisturbed.

MOON

Illustrated in Figure 28
MATERIALS
Plaid Gallery Glass Liquid Leading:
  Soft Black

Plaid Gallery Glass Window Colour:
  Sunny Yellow
  White Pearl

plastic A4 sleeve
toothpicks
pin

METHOD
Insert design inside plastic sleeve and outline in Liquid Leading. Allow to dry overnight or until the leading is firm to the touch, then apply Window Colour in the following sequence.

Run a line of White Pearl along inner curved edge of moon.

Squeeze Sunny Yellow over remainder of moon. While both paints are still wet, blend the White Pearl into the Sunny Yellow with a toothpick, using a backwards and forwards motion.

If paint goes over eye and mouth, don't worry, as these details will show up when paint dries to a transparent finish.

Use a pin to burst any air bubbles.

Set aside to dry for 24 to 48 hours. When the paint is completely dry, gently peel the moon off the plastic and attach it to a clean glass or tile surface, pressing from the top downwards, applying firm pressure to remove any air from underneath. It will remain firmly fixed if left undisturbed.

SUN

Illustrated in Figure 28
MATERIALS
Plaid Gallery Glass Liquid Leading:
  Soft Black
Plaid Gallery Glass Window Colour:
  Sunny Yellow
  Ruby Red
plastic A4 sleeve
toothpicks
pin

METHOD
Insert design inside plastic sleeve and outline in Liquid Leading. Allow to dry overnight or until the leading is firm to the touch, then apply Window Colour in the following sequence.

Colour centre circle of sun with Sunny Yellow.

Colour outer spikes with Sunny Yellow plus a dot of Ruby Red at inner edge. Use a toothpick or pin to streak the Ruby Red into the Sunny Yellow.

Use a pin to burst any air bubbles.

Set aside to dry for 24 to 48 hours. When completely dry, gently peel the sun off the plastic and attach it to a clean glass or tile surface, pressing from the top downwards, applying firm pressure to remove any air from underneath. It will remain firmly fixed if left undisturbed.

SUNCATCHERS

These colourful suncatchers can be created by working onto acetate, but the same designs can also be used as peel and press elements using Window Colour on A4 plastic sleeves.

You could also use these circular designs to decorate glass canisters, following the method described for the Australian native flower canisters on pages 24–28.

A4-sized sheets of acetate are sold at stationers for use as overhead transparency sheets. Two of these designs will fit onto one acetate sheet.

Once the paint has completely dried, cut around the outer border and pierce the top of the suncatcher using a fine needle and thread. Knot the ends of the thread together and hang your suncatchers from windows or light fittings.

I have created a finer appearance by sitting the paint tubes in a cup of hot water before use, making the paint more fluid and easier to spread. Once the paint has been pushed to meet the edge of the leading, use a pin to comb through the wet paint to give a less textured finish.

YELLOW FISH

Illustrated in Figure 29
MATERIALS
1 sheet acetate (overhead transparency sheet)
Plaid Gallery Glass Liquid Leading:
  Soft Black
Plaid Gallery Glass Window Colour:
  Sunny Yellow
  Kelly Green
  Emerald Green
  Royal Blue
  Blue Diamond
  Crystal Clear
pin

METHOD
Place design underneath acetate and use Liquid Leading to outline design.

To make the finer line to outline the eye, modify the nozzle with the sticky tape extension described on page 4. Set aside to dry for 12 to 24 hours. Apply Window Colour paint in the following sequence.

Body Leaving the outer eye area free of paint, colour main part of the body and half of the tail in Sunny Yellow. Comb through with a pin. While yellow is still wet, squeeze on Royal Blue spots as indicated in photograph.

Fins Colour the fins and the outer edge of the tail in Royal Blue. Comb through with a pin.

Reeds Alternate between Kelly Green and Emerald Green to colour the reeds, as in the photo. Comb through with a pin.

Background Use a mix of 3 parts Crystal Clear and 1 part Blue Diamond. It is easier to add a small amount of Blue Diamond to a bottle of Crystal Clear and mix with a skewer to combine colours. Once applied, comb through with a pin.

Burst any air bubbles with a pin and leave to dry on a flat surface before cutting out and hanging as described above.

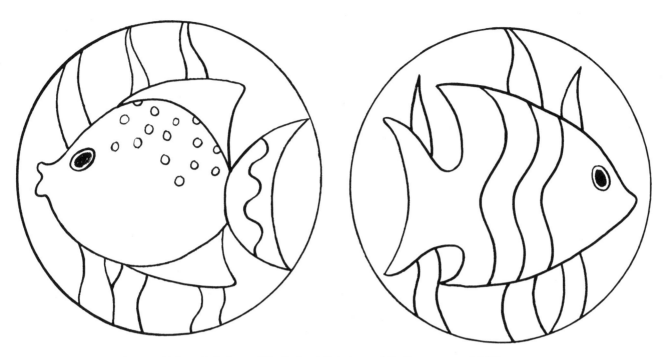

ABOVE: Suncatcher designs: Yellow Fish (page 52), Striped Fish (page 54). **ENLARGE AT 161%**

BELOW: Suncatcher designs: White Daisy (page 54), Orange Tiger Lily (page 55). **ENLARGE AT 161%**

STRIPED FISH

Illustrated in Figure 30
MATERIALS
1 sheet acetate (overhead transparency sheet)
Plaid Gallery Glass Liquid Leading:
 Soft Black
Plaid Gallery Glass Window Colour:
 Amethyst
 Magenta Royale
 Emerald Green
 Kelly Green
 Blue Diamond
pin

METHOD
Place design underneath acetate and use Liquid Leading to outline design. To make the finer line to outline the eye, modify the nozzle with the sticky tape extension described on page 4. Set aside to dry for 12 to 24 hours.

Apply Window Colour paint in the following sequence.

Body Use Amethyst to colour the first stripe and the tail area of the fish. Colour the other stripe with Magenta Royale. Comb through with a pin before squeezing spots of Magenta Royale on Amethyst sections (refer to photo).

Head Leaving the outer eye area free of paint, colour the head area with Magenta Royale. Comb through with a pin.

Reeds Colour the first reed with Kelly Green, the second reed with Emerald Green and the third reed with Kelly Green. Comb through with a pin.

Background Paint with Blue Diamond and comb through with a pin.

Burst any air bubbles with a pin and leave to dry on a flat surface before cutting out and hanging as described above.

WHITE DAISY

Illustrated in Figure 31
MATERIALS
1 sheet acetate (overhead transparency sheet)
Plaid Gallery Glass Liquid Leading:
 Soft Black
Plaid Gallery Glass Window Colour:
 Snow White
 Sunny Yellow
 Kelly Green
 Crystal Clear
 Emerald Green
 Blue Diamond
toothpicks
pin

METHOD
Place design underneath acetate and use Liquid Leading to outline design.

Set aside to dry for 12 to 24 hours.

Apply Window Colour in the following sequence.

Flower Colour centre of daisy with Sunny Yellow. Colour petals with Snow White, comb through with a pin, and while white is still wet, squeeze a dot of Emerald Green at the inner edge of each petal. Use a pin to streak this colour into the Snow White (refer to photo).

Leaves and stem Use a mix of 2 parts Crystal Clear and 1 part Kelly Green on the upper half of each leaf, and Kelly Green on the lower halves and the stem. Combine colours with a toothpick. Comb through with a pin.

Background Use Blue Diamond and Emerald Green to colour opposite quarters of background. Comb through with a pin.

ORANGE TIGER LILY

Illustrated in Figure 32
MATERIALS
1 sheet acetate (overhead transparency sheet)
Plaid Gallery Glass Liquid Leading:
 Soft Black
Plaid Gallery Glass Window Colour:
 Orange Poppy
 Emerald Green
 Kelly Green
 Crystal Clear
 Sunny Yellow
toothpicks
pin

METHOD
Place design underneath acetate and use Liquid Leading to outline design.
 Set aside to dry for 12 to 24 hours.

Apply Window Colour in the following sequence.

Petals Squeeze Orange Poppy into each petal section and comb through with a pin.

Stem Colour stem with Emerald Green and comb through with a pin.

Background Use a mix of 2 parts Crystal Clear and 1 part Kelly Green (combining colours with a toothpick), to colour two sections of the background, and Sunny Yellow to colour the other two sections.

Burst any air bubbles with a pin and leave to dry on a flat surface before cutting out and hanging as described above.

FULL BUTTERFLY

Illustrated in Figure 33
MATERIALS
1 sheet acetate (overhead transparency sheet)
Plaid Gallery Glass Liquid Leading:
 Soft Black
Plaid Gallery Glass Window Colour:

Snow White
Berry Red
Blue Diamond
Denim Blue
toothpicks
pin

METHOD

Place design underneath acetate and use Liquid Leading to outline design.

Set aside to dry for 12 to 24 hours.

Apply Window Colour in the following sequence.

Body Colour with Denim Blue. Comb through with a pin.

Wings Apply Berry Red on inner wing area, against body, then apply Blue Diamond. Use a pin to streak backwards and forwards to graduate the colour, using the photo for guidance. On outer edge of wing, squeeze Snow White with a few drops of Berry Red. Use a toothpick to blend colours together and comb through with a pin. While paint is still wet, squeeze on spots of Berry Red (refer to photo).

Background Colour with Snow White. Comb through with a pin.

Burst any air bubbles with a pin and leave to dry on a flat surface before cutting out and hanging as described above.

HALF BUTTERFLY

Illustrated in Figure 34
MATERIALS

1 sheet acetate (overhead transparency sheet)
Plaid Gallery Glass Liquid Leading:
  Soft Black
Plaid Gallery Glass Window Colour:
  Snow White
  Berry Red
  Blue Diamond
toothpicks
pin

METHOD

Place design underneath acetate and use Liquid Leading to outline design.

Set aside to dry for 12 to 24 hours.

Apply Window Colour in the following sequence.

Body Colour with a mix of equal amounts of Snow White and Berry Red, using a toothpick to combine. Comb through with a pin.

Wings Colour main wing area with Snow White and comb through with a pin, then squeeze a tiny dot of Blue Diamond at inner edge of each wing section. Use a pin to streak the blue softly into the white.

Colour outer wing edge with Berry Red, comb through with a pin and, while paint is still wet squeeze drops of Snow White over the top.

Background Colour with Blue Diamond and comb through with a pin.

Burst any air bubbles with a pin and leave to dry on a flat surface before cutting out and hanging as described above.

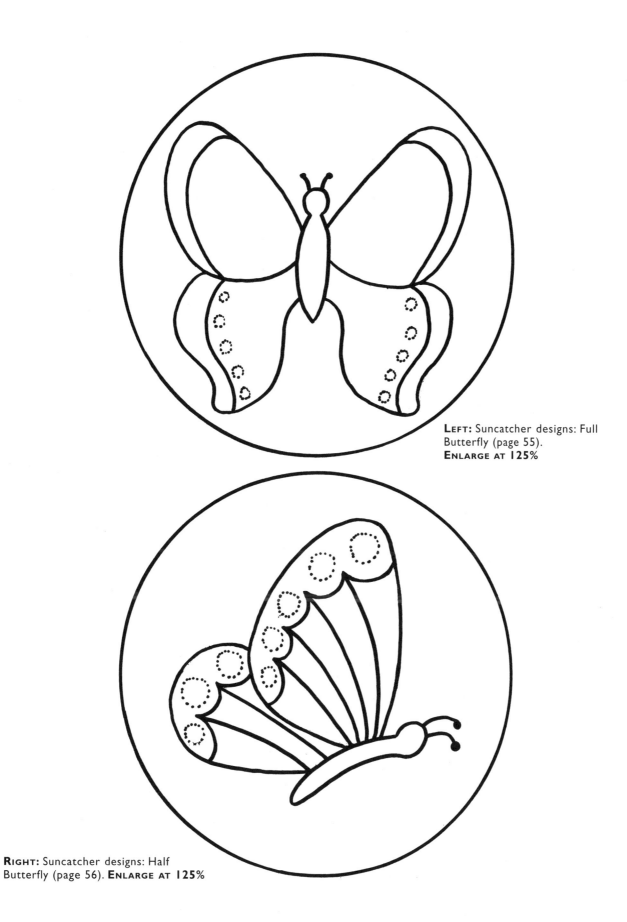

Left: Suncatcher designs: Full Butterfly (page 55). **Enlarge at 125%**

Right: Suncatcher designs: Half Butterfly (page 56). **Enlarge at 125%**

57

INDEX